THE
KERRY
GIRLS

THE
KERRY
GIRLS

Emigration and the Earl Grey Scheme

Kay Moloney Caball

First published 2014

The History Press Ireland
50 City Quay
Dublin 2
Ireland
www.thehistorypress.ie

British Library Cataloguing in Publication Data.
A catalogue record for this book is available from the British Library.

ISBN 978 1 84588 831 2

Typesetting and origination by The History Press

CONTENTS

ACKNOWLEDGEMENTS

I HAVE MANY PEOPLE to thank: those who helped me in my research, in writing and finally in publishing this book.

From the day I started, I had the backing and encouragement of Jimmy Deenihan, Minister for Arts, Heritage & the Gaeltacht, and Chair of the National Famine Commemoration Committee. Jimmy has been deeply committed to all Famine research and publications. He would of course have a particular interest in telling the story of the ancestors of his neighbours and community in Kerry.

The idea for the book was planted during my time studying History of Family and Genealogical Methods at the University of Limerick, with Dr David Butler and Lorna Moloney. The enthusiasm of my classmates there was an inspiration to pursue further research. In particular, Martina Flynn read chapters, criticised and suggested improvements and provided sympathy when needed.

John Pierse and Michael Guerin, mentioned in my Introduction, were the original sources of information on the Famine era in North Kerry. Practical help in accessing the four Board of Guardian Minute books at the Kerry County Archives was provided by Michael Lynch, County Archivist. The National Library was a valuable resource. Further advice and help came from my friends in the Institute of Technology Tralee. Mary Cogan (Listowel Connection) was always there with a wise ear and a sympathetic word when times got difficult. Presbyteries in Dingle, Listowel, Kenmare, Killarney and Ballylongford provided generous co-operation.

I could not have completed the Australian chapters without the help of Julie and Glynn Evans, Sydney, Noni Rush, Newcastle and Gayle Dowling of Melbourne. I was lucky enough to be able to read the contemporary account of the Dingle & Listowel girls' voyage on the *Thomas Arbuthnot* and their subsequent trek through New South Wales to Yass, in the Charles Edward Strutt Journal, October 1849–May 1850, held in the Manuscripts Collection of the State Library of Victoria.

When I finished the book and wondered what to do next, Bridget Kennelly was most helpful and informative. This leads me to Beth Amphlett, my editor at The History Press Ireland, a calm professional who took the work to its publication.

My husband Arthur, whose eyes glaze over when he hears a mention of 'Kerry orphans', deserves thanks for his patience in accompanying me to presbyteries, graveyards, schools and anywhere in the kingdom that might throw light on the background of my subjects.

Finally, to my daughter-in-law Carol Baxter who set me off originally down this path of genealogy and history, a grateful thanks.

INTRODUCTION

I GREW UP IN Listowel, County Kerry and went to school just ninety-six years after the Famine. My school was a few hundred yards from where the Listowel Union Workhouse was situated. Yet I never heard of the Earl Grey Scheme until two or three years ago. In fact, while growing up I heard little or nothing about the Famine or how it affected my locality or the Kerry area in general. It was something that we didn't touch on at school. I thought maybe I was a bad listener and had somehow missed out. But checking with my school friends of the time, they were all either bad listeners, or it was just a part of our history that we were not told about. Why, I ask myself? I still don't have an answer to that question.

The first Famine dedicated local history book I came across was Michael Guerin's *Listowel Workhouse Union* and that led me down the path to the history of the Famine in north Kerry in particular and the girls who were inmates of that workhouse. From there I expanded my research to take into account all of the girls who left Kerry on the Earl Grey Scheme. Subsequently, when typing up John Pierses' seminal work *Teampall Bán*, I got to learn about all the facets of that time – the misery, deprivation, despair and poverty of those affected, the responsible and irresponsible reactions of all those involved in Irish law-making, the other side to life from 1846–1852, the continuing export of food from Ireland, the race meetings and balls taking place locally in the midst of such desolation.

While the Kerry 'orphans' undoubtedly lived in abject distress prior to and while in the workhouses, it is good to know now that there were supportive and humane people ready to speak up for them, and to help them. From when they were 'selected' by Lieutenant Henry, to the assistance given to them by Surgeon Charles Strutt on the *Thomas Arbuthnot* and again in accompanying many of these girls on the trek to Yass where he insisted on providing good employers for them.

The Kerry girls themselves, whether from Dingle, Kenmare, Killarney or Listowel, showed us what they were made of. They were a courageous, resilient, independent, gutsy and spirited lot. I like to think Kerry girls still display these attributes.

BACKGROUND TO THE FAMINE IN KERRY

K ING WROTE IN his *History of Kerry*, 'During the first half of the nineteenth century distress was the constant condition of the people of Kerry'. The spectre of famine was never far off. In 1821, out of a county population of 230,000, 170,000 were reported to be destitute of the means of subsistence'.[1] It is not surprising then that this endemic poverty, together with the rapid growth in the population and the misguided administration of the British Government over its Irish citizens, lead to the disastrous famine of 1845–1852, a human tragedy of staggering proportions.

During that period hundreds of thousands died of hunger and disease. Hundreds of thousands of Irish emigrated to England, Australia and the Americas. By autumn of 1845 when the Great Famine struck, there were more than 8 million people living on the island of Ireland. The population of Kerry had risen from 216,185 in 1821 to 293,256 in 1841, an alarming 77,071 increase, one of the highest rises in a countrywide population that was escalating rapidly. However, by 1851, after six years of famine resulting in death and emigration, the combined population of the eight baronies that comprised the County of Kerry had dropped to 238,256 in 1851 – a decrease of 55,624 persons in ten years.[2]

While we cannot say with certainty how many people died in Kerry or how many emigrated during the famine period, we know that 117 girls were part of the exodus. They emigrated through the Earl Grey Scheme and came from four of the six Unions in Kerry – Dingle, Kenmare, Killarney and Listowel in 1849 and 1850.

While each of these Union baronies from which the Kerry 'orphans' originated, had its own individual problems and challenges that were responsible for the high death rates and emigration, there were a number of problems common to all geographic areas of the county.

What caused the Great Famine and contributed to its disastrous results? While the loss of the potato crop, which was the main diet of the poor, was the proximate cause, there were a number of other reasons: widespread poverty among the majority, unemployment, overpopulation and an unsatisfactory system of landownership. A Royal Commission set up by the British Government under the Earl of Devon reported in 1845:

> It would be impossible adequately to describe the privations which they [Irish labourer and his family] habitually and silently endure ... in many districts their only food is the potato, their only beverage water ... their cabins are seldom a protection against the weather ... a bed or a blanket is a rare luxury.[3]

In Ireland at this time, the daily intake of a 'third or so of the population was mainly reliant on the potato ... 4-5 kilos daily per adult male equivalent for most of the year'[4] This may seem now like an enormous amount of potatoes for anyone to eat in one day but washed down with buttermilk it was in fact a very healthy diet.

> The nutritional content of the potato and widespread access to heating fuel in the form of turf, eased somewhat the poverty of Ireland's three million 'potato people', who were healthier and lived longer than the poor in other parts of Europe at the time.[5]

Arthur Young noted in 1779 that the potato was largely responsible for the healthiness of the Irish: 'when I see their well formed bodies ... their men athletic and their women beautiful, I know not how to believe them subsisting on an unwholesome food.'[6] John Pierse, in his book *Teampall Bán*, quotes his ancestor Dr John Church: 'I think they are healthy; I see them sometimes come out in crowds out of the cabins, sometimes perfectly naked, and we have been astonished to see how healthy they are.'[7]

While the loss of the potato crop may have been the immediate cause, too many people on too little land without fixity of tenure contributed to the disaster in no small way.

The colonisation of Ireland began with the Normans' arrival in 1171, but it was in the reigns of Henry VIII, Elizabeth I, Oliver Cromwell and William of Orange that the main confiscation of Irish land took place. Irish lands were granted by the Crown to English or Scottish planters. These new planters, of English stock with a Protestant identity then became powerful landlords over vast tracts of land.

In 1695 harsh Penal Laws were introduced. Irish Catholics who had been dispossessed of their own land were then prohibited from buying land, bringing their children up as Catholics, from entering the forces or the professions. Neither could Catholics, Jews, Protestant Dissenters (non-Anglicans) and Quakers run for elected office or own property (such as horses) valued at more than £5. So, instead of owning land, most rented small plots from absentee British landlords. While tenancy can be a very efficient and fair way to use land, this was not the case in Ireland.

This system of landownership was one of the major causes of poverty. It is estimated that by the time of the Famine, 70–75 per cent of all tenants held land 'at will'[8] and leases were generally short or at most let for one life and twenty-one years, instead of the former system of three lives, with explicit clauses against subletting which in the main were not observed by the tenants. There was little or no security of tenure. By law, any improvements made by the tenant, such as draining the land, building fences or even erecting a stone house, became the property of the landlord. Thus there was never any incentive to upgrade their living conditions. The landlord could also increase the rent if the tenant's 'improvements' warranted it. Tenants could be evicted between leases if the landlord or agent could make more money out of the land themselves, or get a higher rent from another tenant. These landowners, unlike the situation in England, had no link to their tenants save an economic one. They had acquired their estates during the plantations and confiscations over the previous 200 years. One such acquisition was in 1666, when the Provost, Fellows and Scholars of Trinity College, Dublin, were granted 54,479 acres of land in Kerry. By the early 1850s, most of this land was sublet to agents who in turn sublet it to tenants. At the eve of the Famine, Trinity College owned 6.4 per cent of the county.[9]

While the majority of Kerry landlords were absentees, they were represented in the area by these agents or middlemen. In a lot of cases, the latter were more feared than the actual landowner. They managed the estates of the absentees, set the rents, let and sublet the land. They were the ones who had the power to call in the bailiffs, evict tenants and put them on the side of the road.

The tenants were also separated from their landlords by culture, religion, language and a great sense of dispossession. Many of these Catholic tenants were now paying rent to families who had driven their ancestors out of the land they had previously owned for generations. On their part, the landlords did not have a great sense of security and did not relish living among what they saw as a disgruntled, unreliable peasantry. As a result, the major landowners lived elsewhere, some in other parts of Ireland but mostly in England. Rents collected to fund their extravagant lifestyles on their English estates were the main objective of this landowning class.

An addition to the landownership problems was the practice of subdivision. By 1841, the growth in population, resulting from marriage at a younger age, meant that land distributed among a number of sons, over a couple of generations, led to each holding becoming smaller and smaller until it was barely enough to support a family.

Social and living conditions in Kerry in the first half of the nineteenth century were diverse and wide ranging. At the top of the social ladder you had the aforementioned landlords, living outside the county, where they looked after their other estates, their commissions in the (British) army and/or their seats in Parliament. Next you had a slowly emerging merchant class in the towns, who lived in substantial houses with servants and a prosperous lifestyle. These were mostly Protestant, but since the Repeal of the Penal Laws in 1782, a Catholic minority of business people was emerging. In the country you had a small number of 'strong farmers', those who held 30 acres or more. Survivors of the famine, who were interviewed in the 1920s by Bryan MacMahon all agreed that 'comfortable' farmers were not in serious distress during these times.[10]

The average tenant farmers were those with between 5 and 30 acres. On this acreage they were living at subsistence level. Then you had the cottiers and labourers, who were the most numerous, and it was this section of the community who were wiped out during the Famine. A cottier or labourer might have half an acre, where he would grow potatoes and build a cabin. He would pay the farmer for the land, usually about £5 (1800s) or, more often, with his labour. This plot of ground was an essential need; without it he starved. These cottiers and labourers usually kept a pig and hens and most lived in one-roomed mud houses without windows or chimney. The 1841 Census classification distinguished between four types of houses. Fourth-class houses were defined as 'all mud cabins having only one room'.[11]

> Imagine four walls of dried mud (which the rain, as it falls, easily restores to its primitive condition) having for its roof a little straw or some sods, for its chimney a hole cut in the roof, or very frequently the door through which alone the smoke finds an issue. A single apartment contains father, mother, children and sometimes a grandfather and a grandmother; there is no furniture in the wretched hovel; a single bed of straw serves the entire family.[12]

These labourers and cottiers in Kerry at this time had a very low standard of living. They were poorly clothed and very few had shoes. A detailed enquiry into rural poverty reported in 1836 that an agricultural labourer could, on average, count on 134 days of paid employment in a year.

The cottier or labourer would have married young, men at 18 or 19 and girls at 16 or 17, and had a large family. The labourer's children, mostly the males, who did not get settled on their parents subdivided acreage, would offer their services as '*spailpíns*' at hiring fairs to strong farmers in other parts of the country, in particular West Limerick and Cork, or they would attempt to emigrate if at all possible. There was little or no opportunity for paid work, or indeed apprenticeships, open to women. Their living conditions would not have equipped them with the experience for the usual housekeeping duties that would have led to employment with the merchant class or the 'Big House'.

We know from the 1841 Census that male illiteracy topped 60 per cent on a countrywide basis. This figure would then be higher for females, as education for girls would not have been regarded as a priority by parents. Girls would be 'kept at home' in greater numbers to look after younger siblings, assisting with the daily farming – digging potatoes, footing turf, helping with any harvesting, baking bread and boiling potatoes, sewing and washing whatever few clothes they had in nearest streams or rivers.

The difficulties of isolated communities and lack of financial resources affected the attendance of pupils at 'pay schools' as they were known, which existed in most areas in the early half of the nineteenth century. They had started as traditional 'hedge schools' where classes were held outdoors in the bogs and corners of fields, in order to avoid detection by the authorities during the times of the Penal Laws when education was banned for the Catholic community. These 'pay schools' were now settled in permanent outhouses or cabins and as the name suggests, the pupils paid a fee to the teacher. Families were willing to pay these small sums if they could at all afford them, to have their children learn not just the usual reading, writing, arithmetic, history, geography, all through the medium of Irish, but for some of the more advanced pupils – from families of the merchant class or strong farmers – the rudiments of Greek and Latin, in private schools in the towns in Tralee, Killarney or Listowel. In 1831 the National Education Board was established by the Government 'for the education of the poor in Ireland' and from early 1840s the hedge schools were gradually replaced by free national education. This education was through the medium of English and had both cultural and language challenges.

In North Kerry, Slieveadara National School opened on 1 December 1843, replacing the existing Ardoughter Hedge School. While this new school was well built in stone and slated, multi-denominational and free, these National Schools were not without their problems. All instruction was to be given through English even though the first pupils were not used to reading English, 'as the little English they possessed was oral, and they had seldom if ever seen the written English script'.[13] Each pupil was to commit to memory the following 'poem' and it was recited every morning:

I thank the goodness and the grace,
Which on my birth has smiled
And made me in these Christian times,
A happy English child.[14]

While some of the families would have been able to read or read and write, most would have spoken either Irish or a Kerry version of Hiberno-English. Although the Irish language had started to decline by 1845, about 30 per cent were speaking Irish on the eve of the Famine, it was disproportionately those who spoke Irish as their daily tongue who died or emigrated.

Dingle Union

The Dingle Peninsula itself suffered much death and starvation from 1845 onwards and there were specific reasons for this. The Peninsula of Corkaguiny was made up of 'several wretched villages'[15] with densely populated coastal communities and one main urban centre – the town of Dingle itself.

These 'wretched villages' were in fact groups of small cabins and huts clustered together in what were called *clacháns*. They were composed of families and their few animals, generally on very poor stony or boggy land, trying to eke a living.

There was no one focal point with the exception of Dingle itself, which had very poor communication links to the rest of the county. Dingle was 30 miles from Tralee over backbreaking, and in winter impassable, mountain boreens and was 10 miles from Ballyferriter or Dunquin over unmade roads. In December of 1847, the Dingle Guardians on the Board of the Tralee Poor Law Union petitioned for a temporary workhouse to be set up in Dingle. This was to be 'for the reception of the poor now reduced to such a state of hunger and weakness as to render them perfectly unable to travel to Tralee'. De Moleyns, the principal landlord, also pointed out regarding the peninsula that 'not a single magistrate or gentleman of property resided within it; and that co-operation between Catholic and Protestant clergy was highly unlikely since conversions from amongst the lower orders had brought about a state of religious warfare'.[16] The vast majority of the population of Corkaguiny spoke Irish as their first, and in most cases only, language, which created another communication barrier between them and the Poor Law Guardians in Tralee as well as with the representative of the Poor Law Commissioners in Dublin.

Corkaguiny had two major landlords: Richard Boyle, 9th Earl of Cork, and Thomas Townsend Aramberg De Moleyns, Lord Ventry. *The Times* of London on 6 January 1849 published a column entitled 'Evictions in Dingle', quoting the *Limerick Chronicle* and detailing recent evictions carried out by Lord Ventry: 'Total of recent evictions from Lord Ventry's property near Dingle, 170 families, 532 souls ... have been ejected by a posse of bailiffs acting under the power of English law.'[17]

Lord Cork owned land in almost all parishes in the Barony of Corkaguiny, including the Blasket Islands, at the time of Griffith's Valuation, as well as in other parts of Kerry. Lord Ventry, whose house was at Burnham was for the most part an absentee landlord. Lewis mentions that the family lived for much of the time in England and the house was occupied by their agent, David Thompson.[18] Ventry Estates was in trust in chancery for the forty-one years in which Thomas Townsend Aremberg de Moleyns held the title – from 1827 to 1868. This 3rd Baron Ventry was absent for many of the earlier years and was wounded in the Peninsular War. He was disabled when he returned. Because of his injuries his tenants knew him as 'An Tiarna Bacach' (the Lame Earl).

From 1833 onwards a proselytising campaign was launched on the Dingle Peninsula and it was the one successful protestant missionary effort in Kerry. Lord Ventry, his wife Eliza and the Agent David Thompson were most active in pressurising Catholics to convert to Protestantism. David Thompson was able to exert pressure on tenants when setting rents – lower rents would be offered to those who would convert. Revd Charles Gayer, who arrived in Dingle in 1833 as private chaplain to Lord Ventry, is the name most associated now with the Famine Proselytising Campaign.

Protestant colonies and school houses were established in Dunquin, the Great Blasket Island, Dunurlin, Kilmalkedar and Ventry. Twenty Irish-speaking teachers were sent to the area. Two notable convertees from a Roman Catholic family who were very influential in alerting the authorities to the impending doom were Matthew Trant Moriarty and his brother Thomas. While at school Thomas and his family came under the influence of his Protestant Irish teachers, prompting three of the Moriarty brothers – Matthew, Thomas and Denis – to become clergymen of the Church of Ireland. Matthew T. resided at Ventry during the Famine and was one of the first to give a voice and highlight the increasing distress.[19] From 1845 onwards he was writing to the *Kerry Evening Post*, initially forecasting and then describing the horror in February 1847:

Picture to yourself ... a Parish, with all its villages depopulated by emigration to eternity or America, many of its wives and children deserted; all its fields uncultivated; the hearts and hopes of many yet in it broken; it's Church-yard filled – that is Ventry.[20]

Between 700 and 800 destitute people converted to the Church of Ireland, many of whom reverted later. The issue of soup to the poor was used during the years 1846–1851 to convert Catholics to the Established Church. Those who 'took the soup' were called 'Soupers' and it is a term still used today. Lady Ventry, assisted by Mrs Hickson and Mrs Hussey, established one of the earliest soup kitchens and they distributed one pint of soup per person each morning.

The *Kerry Examiner* of 8 February 1847 records:

The state of the people in Dingle is horrifying. Fever, famine and dysentery are daily increasing, deaths from hunger daily occurring. From all parts of the country, they crowd into the town for relief and not a pound of meal is to be had in the wretched town for any price.

Men who come home from the [public] work die almost and suddenly; and are often left three or four days waiting to see if their friends could scrape together the price of a coffin, and sometimes in vain.[21]

More people died from disease – hunger, typhus, tuberculosis, scurvy, bronchitis, pneumonia and cholera – than actual hunger in the Dingle Workhouse. The *Kerry Evening Post* of January 1847 reported:

Starvation ... fever and dysentery are doing their work here. Six persons died in one lane in this town [Dingle] in one day. The dead are now buried without coffins. Whole villages to the west are in fever. It is almost deplorable to hear the children crying at every corner of hunger ... The people are dying particularly to the west of Dingle by wholesale of starvation, fever and dysentery.[22]

Temporary fever hospitals had been set up in Dingle and Castlegregory It is estimated that up to 5,000 people died and were buried in paupers' graves at the foot of Cnoc a'Chairn, which overlooks Dingle town.

Catherine Moriarty

Catherine Moriarty was born in Dingle, County Kerry, on 17 March 1831 to Maurice Moriarty and Margaret Cahalane, who had married at St Mary's Church, Dingle on 21 February 1827. A brother John had been born on 31 May 1828, a sister Mary on 8 April 1833 and a brother James on 28 February 1836, all at Dingle. No records have been found about these brothers.

Mike Vincent, Catherine's great-great-grandson, tells us:

By 1849 the Moriarty sisters were classified as 'orphans' and were residing in the workhouse in Dingle. They were sent to Australia on the *Thomas Arbuthnot*, arriving in Sydney on February 3, 1850. At this time Catherine and Mary were actually aged 19 and 17 years respectively (the arrival records are 17 and 16). Catherine could neither read nor write, but Mary was able to read. After a short stay in Sydney they moved to Brisbane, on the steamer *Tamar*, and after 13 days Catherine was employed by John Bruce at North Brisbane. By the 9th of June 1852 Mary had met and married James (Samuel) Brassington, a resident of Ipswich. Catherine was a witness at her sister's ceremony in St. Stephen's Catholic Church, Brisbane. On June 7, 1853 Thomas Elliott and Catherine were married. They returned to live in Ipswich where their first child was born on June 7, 1854, and baptised Thomas James at St. Mary's Church.

Catherine's husband, Thomas John Elliott, apprenticed to a tailor at 15 years of age, was found guilty at Westminister Assizes of 'larceny from the person', as pickpocketing was then known, and was sentenced to imprisonment for four months. Baptised Thomas James Elliot on 16 August 1818, at St Clement Danes Church, London, his parents were James Elliot and Mary Ann Whitaker. He was caught again for pickpocketing, tried in the Westminster Sessions on 25 June 1835, and acquitted for lack of evidence. However, on a third occasion, though calling himself James Elliott, his previous conviction was noted, and he was again found guilty of 'larceny from the person' in the Central Criminal Court, Middlesex, on 15 August 1836. Since he had a previous conviction, he was sentenced to fourteen years' transportation. He was held in prison until, on 29 March 1837, along with 199 other convicts, he sailed in the 403-ton barque *Lloyds* and arrived at Port Jackson, Australia, on 17 July 1837.

Thomas was then assigned to work for Charles Kelly at Ham Common in the Windsor district of New South Wales. By 1841 it seems he had left the employ of Kelly, and in 1848 was residing in the Parramatta District when granted his first ticket of leave, on 31 May. He must have been somewhat successful in Sydney, probably as a tailor, for by November 1852 he was working as a tailor in the town of Ipswich, to the west of Moreton Bay. At this time still holding a ticket of leave, he was arrested for some unknown minor offence and sentenced to a month in Brisbane prison, being released on 18 December for 'good conduct' after serving three weeks. He returned to Ipswich where he was soon to meet his future wife, the young Catherine Moriarty.

Thomas's business must have been successful, for between 1854 and 1874 it was able to support his wife and eight children and allow him to purchase and improve various properties around the municipality. Founding his business in the very early days of the town must have helped establish his reputation as a tailor, for he did not advertise in the local paper, the *Queensland Times*, nor anywhere else, so he must have relied on word of mouth and the passing customers for his trade. By 1861 the Elliotts were living in Waghorn Street and renting premises for the tailoring business in Bell Street (later called Union Street). They also invested in land and property in the town and rented out houses they had built. The tailoring business was continued in Union Street until moving to premises in East Street in 1874.

His tailoring business also provided training for his elder daughters, while his contacts enabled his youngest daughter, Elizabeth, to obtain employment at Cribb and Foot's dressmaking department, where by 1906 she was supervisor. Tailoring and dressmaking became traditional family skills for which even his granddaughters were noted.

Thomas decided to leave the tailoring trade, and to retire to the more comfortable hotel accommodation business. Ipswich had always been a centre for accommodation and hotels, and in 1859 for example, when Brisbane had eighteen hotels, Ipswich could boast twenty-six. To this end, in 1874 he obtained a hotel licence after some preliminary purchase, the family eventually rented and ran the One Mile Hotel. This old brick building pound overlooked the One Mile Bridge across the Bremer River. This was the area where in the earliest days of Ipswich the bullock wagons halted on their journeys to and from the Darling Downs.

By 1878, with nine unmarried offspring ranging in age from 2 to 24 years, the family had sufficient experience, confidence and staff to invest in the hotel business. They took out a mortgage for £200, at 10 per cent interest, with the newly formed Ipswich and West Moreton Permanent Building, Benefit and Investment Society, on 5 February, to build a wooden hotel called The Prince of Wales Hotel on the Brisbane Street land, purchased four years before.

One young lad, Bernard Gallagher, had come down from the Bundaberg district to begin work in the Railway Department at Ipswich. His mother (possibly another Irish orphan?) wrote to Catherine Elliott asking her to look after him while staying at their hotel. His stay was worthwhile, for in 1882 he married the Elliotts' second eldest daughter, Margaret Jane, and his job in the railway became a lifelong career, in which he became supervisor of railway stores in Queensland. At least three other daughters, Mary, Elizabeth and Catherine also married railway employees, while all three Elliott sons began their careers in the railway as well.

It is also of interest that two children married into hotel families. Catherine into the Real family, who had hotels and shops in Ipswich, and George into the Lynch family, who at one time held the licence of The Bull's Head Inn, at Drayton.

At the end of 1879 the licence of the Prince of Wales was not renewed, and until 1888 the building in Brisbane Street was operated as a boarding house, but with Tom's failing health, the Elliotts' financial circumstances declined during the 1880s, and they found it necessary to secure additional mortgages on the Brisbane Street property from the Building Society.

Catherine in old age. (Courtesy of Mike Vincent)

This photograph, showing some members of the family, was taken about 1886 by George Patrick Elliott. Seated are the parents, Thomas James and Catherine (Moriarty). Standing are some of their children. From left to right they are (most likely) John Alexander, Margaret Jane (Gallagher), Agnes, Thomas James junior, and Catherine. The location is probably the rear of the Canning Street residence. (Copied from original glass negative in the possession of Monica Elliott, of Brisbane, granddaughter of George Patrick Elliott)

When Tom died of cancer of the jaw at his Canning Street residence in August 1888, his will was proved for probate, leaving all his possessions and property to his wife Catherine, valued at £256, she signed an affidavit stating that at the time of his death he had less than £10 in cash. The mortgage figures and rate arrears indicate that this was probably a fair assessment of his financial situation. Catherine retained possession of the Canning Street home and the boarding-house, which continued to operate. She was now responsible for five daughters and two sons, between the ages of 8 and 23 years, and though some of them were employed and she obtained a loan for £60 in 1889, there were still rates of £7 15s 7d and £11 18s 7d owing on the two properties in 1890.

During the next two decades, daughter Lucy entered the Sacred Heart Convent at Dalby, and the other children were married, most moving away from Ipswich. The Canning Street residence was sold about 1900 and Catherine later moved into a house in Martin Street with her youngest daughter, Elizabeth O'Grady, who had married in 1908. (It was here that Catherine died as a result of a gastric infection in August 1909.) On her death the boarding house passed into the possession of the Ipswich Building Society.

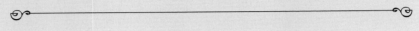

Kenmare

The major problems contributing to the devastation in Kenmare during the Great Famine stemmed in the main from its geographic isolation, its absentee landlord and the population explosion in subdivided land. The remoteness of Kenmare, the relatively small number of Protestant residents or officialdom, had contributed in the previous generation to a general disregard for the law. A 'blind eye' had been turned to the vigorous smuggling trade carried on in the area, and later middlemen, both Protestant and Catholic, had likewise ignored the stipulations in leases regarding the subdivision of landholdings. Communication by road was very difficult. As late as 1828, Kenmare to Derrynane was seven hazardous hours on horseback and, according to Daniel O'Connell, best approached by Killarney or by sea. Only in 1841 was the suspension bridge was erected over the Kenmare River, replacing a ferryman.

The Marquess of Lansdowne's estate amounted to over 94,000 acres in county Kerry, mostly in the Kenmare area. This estate owes its origins to Sir William Petty. He was granted extensive lands in South Kerry, formerly the property of the O'Sullivans, in the seventeenth century. These extensive landholdings then passed through his daughter Anne Petty, who married Thomas Fitzmaurice, 1st Earl of Kerry, and then through their grandson, William Petty-Fitzmaurice.[23]

In Kenmare, Lord Landsdowne's estates had been badly but charitably run by his agent James Hickson for a number of years. He never took on the challenge of subdivision of holdings that was endemic in this area and which in a previous generation had been encouraged by the estate.[24] Hickson, as a result, was a popular agent and was well regarded by the tenantry. This lead to large numbers of families living virtually on top of each other, in cabins grouped together in miserable conditions. Fr John Sullivan of Kenmare told the Devon Commission that the condition of the population was 'very wretched and debased'.[25] William Steurt Trench was appointed the new agent for the Landsdowne Estates in 1849. Having examined the records of the estate he was horrified by the daunting situation. At that time, of the 10,000 paupers then receiving relief in the Union, 3,000 were chargeable to the Landsdowne property. He calculated that maintaining them in the workhouse would cost the estate £5 per head per year when the valuation of the property was barely reaching £10,000 per year.

The living conditions contributed not only to even greater hunger when the potatoes got scarce but it also led to greater risk of disease spreading in this area. The medical officer's report of 22 May 1847 detailed:

> During the past two months the number of those suffering from fever, dysentery and measles averaged 220 per week and 153 inmates died during that period. The workhouse is not only a great hospital for which it was never intended or adapted, but an engine for producing disease and death, as a fearful proportion of the admitted in health fall victim of the fever in a few days due to the crowded state of the house.[26]

Another custom which was peculiar to the area was the migratory habit that not only had the labourers travelling as *spailpíns* to neighbouring counties of Cork, Limerick and Tipperary, but entire families 'nailed up the doors of their huts, took all their children along with them, together with a few tin cans and started on a migratory and piratical expedition over the counties of Kerry and Cork, trusting to their adroitness and good luck in begging to keep the family alive until the potatoes came in again'.[27]

There was an element of proselytising also in the Kenmare area which was reflected in religious strife in the workhouse. In 1850 Denis Mahony of Dromore, who was a minister of the Church of Ireland, established a soup kitchen there and preached to the hungry who came to get some sustenance. This angered the local people, desperate for food. His church was attacked and some of the enraged group then set to uprooting flowerbeds and shrubs in the garden of Dromore House. According to local folklore, it was only through the intervention of Fr John Sullivan that they were stopped as they were about to set fire to the house.

Killarney

While the degree of destitution in Killarney town was great compared to the other Unions in Kerry, the Killarney Board of Guardians functioned best in the Famine years. The main landowners, Lord Kenmare and Henry Arthur Herbert, were resident in the area and the Poor Law Guardians were responsible and committed.

Smith states that Sir Valentine Browne was granted over 6,000 acres in county Kerry after the Desmond Rebellion. Political allegiances in the seventeenth century caused the size of the estate to fluctuate. It was consolidated in the eighteenth century and the Kenmare estate amounted to over 91,000 acres in county Kerry in the 1870s.[28]

By the time of the Famine, Lord Kenmare's land was held predominantly by middlemen. In all his property in Kerry in 1850, the earl had only 300 direct tenants, a very small fraction of the total occupiers.[29] Between 1845 and 1850 Lord Kenmare was able to collect as much as £65,500 out of £93,430, 86 per cent of the rents due.[30] This was achieved without abatements to the middlemen, nor did they default heavily. Rather they squeezed their under-tenants which in turn led to greater poverty and distress among the smaller tenant farmers.

A good example of the subdivision on the Kenmare estates was given by John Leahy of Killarney, in evidence to the Devon Commission, and it clearly outlines the problems subdivision caused both for the tenant and the landlord. He quoted the case of a farm of 30 acres on the Muckross Estate:

> The Lease was made about the year 1800; the rent was £10 Irish. It was let to one tenant but at the time of giving the evidence it had twelve families occupying it, with an average of six persons in each family, he estimated that there would now be seventy two persons living off it. 'With such a mode of cultivation as there is in this country, this farm could hardly support the population on it.

Henry Arthur Herbert MP, was the other principal lessors of property in the Killarney Poor Law Union. In the 1870s his estate amounted to over 47,000 acres in county Kerry. The centre of this large estate was at Muckross, much of it now included in the Killarney National Park.

The Killarney Board of Guardians had funds and the necessary commercial capability to run the workhouses more efficiently than most. By 1850 they had eventually opened up to eleven auxiliary workhouses. The *Tralee Chronicle* of July 1848 quoted a Poor Law inspector who had visited Killarney Workhouse as saying, 'if it was not the best in Ireland, then it was certainly one of the best'.[31]

From the mid-eighteenth century, Killarney enjoyed a healthy tourist trade and by the time of the Famine international visitors to the town were even enjoying outlying tours of the Ring of Kerry. This trade no doubt helped the merchants of the town and in turn influenced the businesslike running and governance of the Poor Law Union. *Slater's Directory* tells us that there were three hotels in the town by 1846. Slater also states of this time: 'Only Killarney and Tralee were showing signs of prosperity.'[32]

Even earlier than this the *Limerick Chronicle* reported, 'Mr. Jackson, son of the President of America and Louis Napoleon Bonaparte are at the Lakes of Killarney.'[33]

So while Killarney would seem, on the surface, one of the better off areas, this was not the entire story. The main landlords being resident in the area and a thriving tourism business masked the situation of the poor unemployed and uneducated in the lanes of the town. It masked the pressure on the cottier and smallholder from the middleman who must and will collect his rents no matter what.

Ellen Leary

Ellen Leary of Islandmore, Glenflesk was the daughter of Daniel Leary and Julia Healy. Ellen was born on 14 October 1832. Kerry baptismal records show that Ellen had at least one older brother, Denis (b. 1825), and younger siblings Ignatius (b. 1833), Gobnet (b. 1837) and Catherine (b. 1840).

Glenflesk incorporated the ancient parish of Killaha. The ruins of the original church, built around the twelfth century, still stand in the graveyard there and a new church built in 1801 continued in use until 1860. Glenflesk, like all other Kerry areas, suffered greatly during the Famine.

The parish priest, Fr Jeremiah Falvey, died on 28 December 1846 as a result of caring for the sick and dying. Fr Falvey, who lived for some years at Curraglass in the house owned by Patrick O'Donoghue, was evicted by the landlord, Herbert of Muckross, due, it is said, to his having voted or having got the parishioners to vote against the latter. We are told that 'Glenflesk is renowned for the number of priests born in the parish',[34] and indeed Ellen's brother Ignatius later became a priest.

Ellen, together with thirty-four other girls from Killarney Workhouse, travelled initially to Penrose Quay, Cork and from there to Plymouth to join the barque *Elgin*, which had started out from Liverpool initially, on its voyage to Port Adelaide.

Cheryl Ward, of Melbourne, takes up the story of what became of her ancestor:

The ship arrived at the McLaren Wharf, at Port Adelaide on September 10th, 1849. The wharf had only been completed a few weeks before their arrival but port conditions were still very basic. Ships anchored in the river and transferred their passengers and cargo in rowboats. The road to Adelaide was worse than a track and it often took 12 hours to travel the few miles into the city. A spring cart would make the journey for 20 shillings a head and a bullock dray was an alternative at 5 shillings a head but the dray was only marginally better than walking.[35]

Ellen spent the next three years in South Australia.[36] No records have yet been located for her during this period.

She met an Englishman, John Ward, on 19 July 1852 and was married to him by the Revd T.P. Wilson, Minister of St John's Anglican Church, Adelaide. John Ward is described as a labourer. Ellen signed the register with an X.

Ellen and John are noted as being of 'Full Age' on the marriage certificate, but there are the usual age discrepancies. We know from Ellen's baptismal certificate that she was 20 years of age when she married.

At some point after their marriage, between 1852 and 1855, the young couple made their way to Fryers Creek, State of Victoria, where large finds of alluvial gold had been reported in 1851 and it was here that the first of their nine children, John Charles, was born.

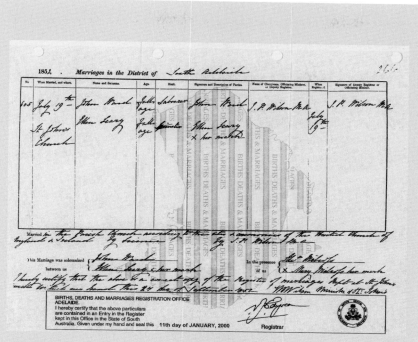

The marriage of Ellen Leary and John Ward, Adelaide, 19 July 1852.

During the gold rush people journeyed, sometimes over vast distances, to and from the diggings. Excited and filled with hope, they made their way to the goldfields by any means available. The trip was difficult, with no made roads to the diggings and crudely constructed river crossings, it could be hot, dry and dusty or wet, muddy and boggy.

Perhaps due to dwindling gold supplies in Fryers Creek, Ellen and John can next be found in Ballarat, where they settled for over a decade and where Ellen was to give birth to a child every second year from 1857 until 1869, with a respite period of four years(!) before their last son, Samuel Ignatius, was born in 1873.

The first evidence we have of Ellen and John in Bairnsdale is in 1885. In 1862 rail lines reached from Melbourne to Gippsland but the gold towns in this area never grew into large provincial cities like Ballarat; however, Bairnsdale was a solidly established gold town.

Ellen died suddenly in Bairnsdale in 1902 at the age of 67. She was survived by John, occupation now listed as grazier, and all but one of her children. Her estate included two allotments of land in the county of

Dargo, one 60 acres including a five-roomed weatherboard house, the other 32 acres, as well as a bank account containing £74.

Curiously the assets were in Ellen's name. John states in probate documents presented to the Supreme Court in 1902, 'I transferred the said allotments as a gift to her and for which she obtained a Certificate of Title in her own name, in the month of May 1885' and '... the money in the savings Bank at Bairnsdale is deposited in her own name and was the proceeds of presents or gifts from myself and her children'. The reason for this is still unclear.

John died ten years later, in 1912. They are buried together in Bairnsdale cemetery.

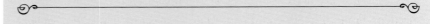

Listowel

Absentee landlords and the middleman system were particularly prevalent in north Kerry. In the Barony of Iraghticonnor, 40,000 acres were owned by Trinity College but leased to middlemen. Other prominent landlords and agents in this area were Lord Listowel and Sir John Benn Walsh together with the Locke Estate (Lady Burghersh), who were all non-resident. Resident landlords and agents included the Crosbies, Stoughtons, Guns, Sandes, St John Blacker and Pierce Mahony, who were mostly in control of lesser lands.

In the 1824 minutes of the evidence put before a Select Committee on the Disturbances in Ireland, chaired by the Right Honourable Lord Viscount Palmerson, Dr John Church said:

> I have known a farm that has been let perhaps thirty years ago to one tenant, to a single individual, and when it was out of lease, and came into possession of the landlord, I have known it to be covered over thick with population, and most of them paupers. It is a very puzzling thing to know what to do with the poor people in such cases.[37]

Evictions in North Kerry contributed in no small way to the number dispossessed who had no option but to make their way to the workhouse in order to have a roof over their heads. In an article by Tim P. O'Neill on Famine evictions,[38] he mentions Kerry in a number of places. The article goes into great detail in relation to the law on evictions. He states, '551 families were cleared from the Trinity College Estates in Kerry, while 16 families were cleared from Commonage in Kerry and their houses levelled.'

Sir John Benn Walsh, who owned extensive estates in North Kerry as well as in Radnorshire in Wales, visited his Kerry properties regularly and kept a journal of his tours. He made an address to the British House of Commons on 7 February 1849, explaining his actions regarding his Listowel Estates, and on 8 September 1851, Benn Walsh stated:

> My own estates have been very much weeded both of paupers and bad tenants. This has been accomplished by Matthew Gabbett (his agent), without evictions, bringing in the sheriff or any harsh measures. In fact, the paupers and the little cottiers cannot keep their holdings without the potato and for small sums of £1, £2, and £3 have given me possession in a great many cases when the cabin is immediately levelled. Then to induce the larger farmer to surrender their holdings when they become insolvent, I emigrated several, either with their whole families or in part.[39]

We also have the evidence of Fr Matthias McMahon, parish priest of Ballybunion, who in an extensive letter to *The Nation* in August 1850 claimed:

> The landlords here may be classed among the worst in Ireland, justice and humanity are alike forgotten by them. The most malignant fiend in hell could not evince more indifference for the sufferings of human beings ... Numbers there are in this doomed district who at no distant period shall be pining in a workhouse, or starving, or wandering over their own land and all owing to the barbarity of the landlords.[40]

Fr McMahon goes on to say in regard to the unjust land laws:

> By a system of detestable injustices an incoming tenant will get abatement which if the former got he might hold on respectably. No matter how much of his labour and capital he may have sunk in the land he is cast out without a farthing compensation.

He calls attention in particular to the activities of St John Blacker, middleman in control of the vast acreage of Trinity College, whom he accuses of demolishing an entire village of twenty houses and 'setting the inhabitants adrift'.[41]

We get a very good description from the Listowel area of the actual conditions of fourth-class houses, as listed in the 1841 Census, then occupied by 60 per cent of the population of the county, from Johanna McKenna of Glashnanoon, Lyreacrompane who gave this account to the Schools Folklore Collection in 1937, when she was 78 years old:

> No Slate houses then, no rooms in them – they had the bed in the kitchen. They used to call them '*bothán*s' and if the walls were made of mud as they used to be, they called them '*Bothán na follaicki*'. Sometimes they were made of black sods of bog and then they were called '*na bothán dubha*' and if they were built on a hill, they call it '*mo bothainín dubh an conaic*'. Sometimes the fire was in the corner with a hole on top for a chimney. There was no glass in the windows. They had wire and board they called 'shutters'. The floor was made of mud and they had no half doors. They used turf for fire and a candle for light. They had a board stuck on the wall and put the candle on that. They made the candle themselves.

A butter market was established in Listowel in 1845 and the 'strong' North Kerry farmers continued to send their produce to the Cork Butter Market right through the Famine. According to Charles O'Brien's *Agricultural Survey of Kerry*, in the early 1800s 'Listowel was one of the five major grain centres in the county'[42] and this grain also continued to be exported for the duration of the Famine. According to John Mitchel, quoted by Cecil Woodham-Smith:[43]

> Ireland was actually producing sufficient food, wool and flax, to feed and clothe not nine but eighteen millions of people, yet a ship sailing into an Irish port during the famine years with a cargo of grain was sure to meet six ships sailing out with a similar cargo.

Some of this corn was shipped from Tralee.

So in 1845 we have our large extended impoverished families living in cabins, dependent on their patch of ground to produce enough potatoes to give them three meals a day washed down with buttermilk, sleeping on straw on the bare earth without any work available to the vast majority. We have depended on folklore to tell us that this section of the Kerry population were 'poor but happy'. They understood well that their options of improving their lot were very limited, and led a day-to-day existence. They placed great emphasis on song and dance, on storytelling, and had close relationships with their neighbours and parish. They valued strong ties with their extended families and depended on them for practical and emotional support. They were not lazy, stupid, promiscuous or immoral as they were portrayed in the British media.

We also have a smaller number of 'strong farmers' investing their time, energy and whatever finances are available, working their acreage, improving their living conditions and agricultural holdings, educating their children and reasonably content that their families are aspiring to a better class of life.

Thus were the conditions in Kerry when the potato blight first struck in the autumn of 1845.

Bridget Ryan

Bridget (Biddy) Ryan is one of the intriguing stories of the Earl Grey Orphans' and one we have not solved entirely. When Bridget was originally 'selected' by Lieutenant Henry in Listowel Workhouse, her address on the Minutes on 11 September 1849 was 'Listowel'. However, when she arrived in Sydney on the *Thomas Arbuthnot* on 3 February, she declared her native place as Bruff, Limerick, gave her age as 16, her parents as Anthony and Johanna, and stated that her father (a soldier) was living in Sydney. She was able to read and write. It was noted under 'State of Health, strength and probable usefulness: Poor'.

Bridget's great-great-granddaughters – Julie Evans and Jeanette Greenway have done extensive work to uncover Bridget's family in Ireland and also have provided us with a record of her life in Australia:

Bridget's first employer was a Captain Mac Kellar who was a Master Mariner and originally from Elgin in Scotland. It is not clear how Bridget met her husband James Murray and it may have been through this employer.

James had arrived from Scotland in 1848. Family lore suggests he was working in Sydney at the time, though his brothers were farming in the Manning River area of New South Wales. Bridget and James were married in Sydney in December 1850 and in December 1851 they had the first of their thirteen children (one did not survive infancy). It has been impossible to trace the Australian marriage certificate of James and Bridget and other dated information we have has been obtained from their death certificates.

Roman Catholic Bridget became a Free Presbyterian on her marriage and is reported to have adopted her new faith with great vigour. They were reported as being 'pillars' of their Church and James was a churchwarden for many years.

James and Bridget set up their first home on a farm at Mondrook. After severe floods for three years in a row, they moved to a dairy farm on Oxley Island where they remained until James died in 1893. There are ruined and overgrown remains of the old dairy still on this property but the house is long gone.

The children were brought up strictly in the Presbyterian faith. Four of James and Bridget's children married their cousins, as was common at the time. All their children remained in New South Wales. Descendants of these children have now scattered widely across Australia and overseas.

It is said that when James died in 1893, his casket was brought down the river on a steam tug and taken to Tinonee for the funeral service. James was buried in Tinonee Cemetery. Bridget died in 1909 and was buried beside James.

While Bridget's life in Australia is well documented, it is her history in Ireland that is most intriguing. Thanks to Julie and Jeanette we get a partial and tantalising glimpse to her background in Ireland. This background is the subject of a TG4 Documentary to be shown in October 2013.

From the initial snippets on record that Bridget's father was in Sydney and was a soldier and from her Australian family folklore that she herself

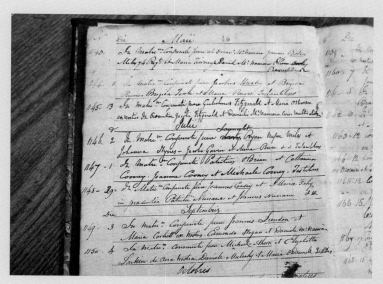

The marriage certificate of Johanna Hynes and Lancelot Ryan, Bruff parish church 1831.

had been educated in Ireland by 'French nuns', we pieced together her background as it was in 1849 when she left Listowel Workhouse.

Bridget's parents were Johanna Hynes and Lancelot 'Lanty' Ryan (not Anthony). Johanna and Lancelot, as he was called on the marriage certificate, were married in Bruff Parish Church on 2 July 1831. Written in Latin, his occupation was given as 'lately a Soldier'.

Searches for Lanty's career as a soldier in Australia didn't realise any results and it transpired that the reality was somewhat different. He had in fact got married again, bigamously, in 1837 in Abbeyfeale, County Limerick and as a result he had been transported as a convict to Australia. The following is an extract from the New South Wales State Records:

Convict List for the Ship Neptune 1837-1838

The vessel departed Dublin 27 August 1837 for the 128 day voyage to Sydney. The prisoner list includes:

Ryan Launcelot, age 35, tried 1837, Limerick 7 yrs, b. 1803 Tipperary, bigamy, married, 1m 1f children, soldier labourer, blind of left eye, CF 44/1140

Lanty tried to make a deal just before the *Neptune* sailed out from Kingstown Harbour in Dublin. He had some involvement or knowledge of an incident in 1831 during the Tithe War in Doon, Co. Limerick, where a number of men had attacked the Rev Charles Coote who was endeavouring to collect the hated Tithes, then due to the Established Church of Ireland by all landholders, most of whom would have been Catholics. A reward was offered for information on the culprits and while Lanty had not made any claim to the money for the previous six years, he now tried to use his information in a last ditch effort to escape transportation. It was too late however, and the ship sailed.

On arrival in Australia, he was noted as having a number of facial injuries, scars, one eye and one arm and as such was of no use as a convict

Bridget Ryan Murray in old age.

Waterview House, Balmain, where Bridget Ryan worked. According to her descendent, Julie Evans, 'the house was leased by the man who employed Bridget in 1850'. (Courtesy of State Library of NSW)

worker in the bush. He seems to have remained in the special compound in Port Maquarie for old, infirm or disabled convicts and it is most unlikely that Bridget ever met him.

Even after extensive research, we have no idea what happened to Johanna or her family in Ireland. Johanna, on the conviction of her husband, would have had only two options open to her – to return to her own family home in Bruff or to seek shelter in one of the workhouses, then in Kilmallock and Limerick. We have to presume that she went back to her family near Lough Gur, and it would appear from Bridget's own story to her children that she herself spent some time as a pupil in Laurel Hill Convent in Limerick, then the only convent with 'French nuns'. This is quite possible as the famous Dean Cussen was then the parish priest of Bruff. He was one of the principal supporters of the sisters in Laurel Hill, who had just opened their school (in 1845) and he may have arranged through the Hynes family (Bridget's grandparents) that Bridget be taken in there.

So how did Bridget, a native of Bruff, end up in the workhouse in Listowel? This is another mystery that probably will not be solved now,

160 years later. According the rules governing the Earl Grey Scheme, 'orphans' to be selected should have been resident in the workhouse for at least one year. My own sense is that a benefactor used his influence with the Board of Guardians to get her away from the wretched circumstances, the poverty and despair that would have been her fate in Ireland. This benefactor may have been Dean Cussen once again.

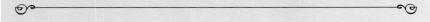

≈2≈

LIFE IN
THE WORKHOUSE

ORKHOUSES CAME TO Ireland as a result of the 1838 Poor
Law enacted in the British Parliament. In 1800, Ireland, under
the Act of Union, became part of Great Britain with the English
Parliament responsible for governing the country. While the government
recognised that there was widespread and dire poverty in the country, their
numerous but feeble attempts to address the problem failed. A number of
Parliamentary Select Committees as well as 114 Royal Commissions and
sixty-one Special Committees of Enquiry which investigated conditions in
Ireland between 1800 and 1840, produced no practical results.[1]

In 1834 the Poor Law Amendment Act was passed for England and
Wales where the only form of poor relief was to be via the workhouse. This
was to stop any malingerers or work-shy people from looking for relief –
their only option to get any sort of help was to enter the workhouse and get
food and shelter there. While the same system was considered initially for
Ireland, it was turned down almost immediately because it was recognised
that there actually was no work available in Ireland – it wasn't a choice of
working or not working that was the problem.

While a number of proposals were considered and abandoned, it wasn't
until 1836 that George Nicholls, an English Poor Law Commissioner, was
sent to Ireland to investigate if the English system, funded by a local poor
rate, would work in Ireland. This system would depend on a workhouse

provision only. After a quick six-week tour of Ireland, he recommended that a similar system to the English one should be adopted. He did not seem to recognise that the causes for the level and depth of poverty in Ireland were totally different to those in England. Daniel O'Connell ridiculed his conclusions, saying, 'He calculated everything and was accurate in nothing'.[2]

The Act proposed was met with dissatisfaction on all sides. The landlords opposed it because of their fears of the costs associated, which would be levied on the poor rate, and the tenants, who had a pathological dread of 'ending up in the workhouse', without any possibility of out-relief in any form, were equally incensed. No provision was made for 'outdoor relief' and there was no 'right' to relief; 'it was to be discretionary and dependent on the availability of workhouse places. If a workhouse was full there was no obligation on the Poor Law to provide alternative relief.'[3]

An architect, George Wilkinson, was immediately employed to draw up plans for workhouses capable of keeping up to 800 inmates. The designs of the buildings were all similar. There were to be separate male and female sides.

By 1845, 123 workhouses had been built. The entire country was divided into Poor Law Unions. The Dingle Peninsula was a very poor area and because of its isolated location had suffered greatly until a decision was taken on 22 February 1848 to establish its own Poor Law Union and to erect a temporary workhouse in the town. The new permanent Dingle Union Workhouse did not open until 1852. Distances involved in the peninsula and the difficulty with communications caused untold distress. Captain Hotham, who had been sent by the Poor Law Commissioners firstly to Tralee and then to Dingle to look into the situation there, reported on these difficulties:

> For instance take the relieving officer of Ventry, which is 33 miles from Tralee. He travels to Tralee on Monday to pass his accounts, Tuesday, he awaits the orders of the Board, Wednesday he returns, Thursday, distributes relief, Friday, attends Committee of Guardians at Dingle, Saturday, received applications, visits houses of applicants, and investigates their cases.[4]

Workhouses were smelly, noisy, unpleasant and unhealthy, trying to cope with too many people, many sharing a bed. Large numbers of the inmates had nothing to do but exist in these demoralising conditions.

Ellen Galvin Dingle

Ellen Galvin was one of the Dingle Workhouse girls who travelled on the *Thomas Arbuthnot*, arriving in Port Jackson on 5 February 1850. Her arrival records tell us that she was 18 years of age, Roman Catholic, 'reads only' and her parents John and Mary were both dead.

Unfortunately, if Ellen's age is correct, it is not possible to get her copy baptismal certificate currently, as all entries in the Dingle Baptismal Registers from 1828 to 1834 are illegible or faded.

We also know that Presentation Sisters arrived in Dingle in 1829 to teach. If Ellen lived within walking distance of the town, she would certainly have got an education and her 'reads only' note on arrival probably signifies that her native townland was in a rural area, where schooling was not available. Dingle Union Workhouse looked after nineteen different townlands from Dunquin in the West to Ballinacourty the East, From Brandon to Inch.

Ellen's descendants, Liz Bonner and Leonie Bedford, have researched her story and relate it here. Ellen was Liz's great-great-grandmother descended through her eldest child, William George Castles, and Leonie was a great-great-grandniece of Ellen.

Ellen was housed at Hyde Park Barracks prior to her departure for Yass on 18 February 1850. Together with 107 other girls, they left by dray in the care of Dr Charles Strutt, who had been the Surgeon Superintendent on the *Thomas Arbuthnot*'s voyage from England. The girls walked on the difficult rough sections and travelled on the drays, where possible, to Yass and then to Gundagai. They were housed in the Yass police horse stables, prior to getting employment in the district. Ellen obtained employment as a house servant for Mr J.C. Welman, in Barwang and was paid £8 a year.

Mr John Cameron Welman, who owned the property of 16,000 acres at Barwang, Galong, New South Wales, was one of three Crown Commissioners of Crown Land for the Lachlan district, which included the districts of Boorowa, Young (Lambing Flat), Galong, and Binalong and was thus a quite important person in the area.

Less than one year after arriving in Australia, Ellen met William Castles and they were married by Fr Patrick Magennis of Yass. They married at Barwang on 16 January 1851 and their abode at the time of the marriage was Mr Welman's Barwang property. William signed his name; Ellen wrote an X. John and Bridget Somers were witnesses to the marriage.

In the following seven years, Ellen had six children and she died on 8 September 1859 while giving birth to her last child, Thomas, who survived. On the death certificate, it states she was 26 years of age, married at 19, had four sons and two daughters living when she died and was born in County Clare, Ireland and had been in New South Wales for seven years. (William Castles, who would have supplied the necessary information for the death certificate, obviously got the 'County Clare' native place incorrect). Ellen was buried at Galong Pioneer Cemetery, 'with no priest or minister present'. No headstone exists there for her, nor is there a mention of her in the Galong Cemetery book. The plot has not been found.

As for William Castles, he had been transported on the *Asia* (departed from Portsmouth, England under Captain Stead on 16 October 1831 arrived Sydney on 13 February 1832) when he was 21. His crime was housebreaking, and he was tried at Oxford Assizes in 13 July 1831 and sentenced to transportation for life. The ship's record states he was a groom from Banbury and born in 1811. He was charged with a companion William Hall that on 7 June 1831 'having burglariously [*sic*] broken and entered the dwelling house of Isaac Smith, at Shetford [*sic*] East. [Shutford] and stolen therefrom a gold watch, a silver watch, a pistol, 20 shillings in money, 4 silver spoons and other articles, his property.'

His pardon, signed by Sir Charles Augustus Fitzroy, was dated 18 February 1849. He is listed as obtaining a licence from the Colonial Treasurer for Depasturing Stock beyond the boundaries of the colony near Yass on 18 January 1837.

In 1855, four years before Ellen died, William Castles purchased 16 acres of land located to the left of the main road the Harden. His property adjoined the Binalong police horse paddock, and runs down the hill towards Balgalai Creek. He seems to have a poor relationship with drink as he was charged with being drunk and disorderly and assaulting Constable William Costello at Yass on 12 April 1853 and fined £1 or seven days in gaol in default.

On or about June 1862 William, aged 45 years, accidentally drowned in a creek (he was drunk coming back to home during a flood. The *Yass Courier* of 21 June 1862 had a small article:

FOUND DROWNED. The body of a man named Castles has been found drowned in the creek at Binalong, near the bridge. Castles had been missing for eight days and it is supposed he got into the creek while under the influence of drink.

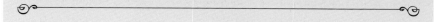

Most people arrived at the workhouse in rags and barefooted. Having gained admittance, the 'pauper' and his family were washed, disinfected and examined by the workhouse doctor for disease, and then 'clothed in a workhouse dress', and the clothes which he wore at the time of his admission 'purified and deposited in a place appropriated for that purpose, with the pauper's name affixed thereto'. Following this procedure was the part most dreaded by all the inmates – families were separated. There were different classifications for different age groups outlined clearly on the rules. Male and female adults were lodged in separate dormitories and children under the age of 2, over the age of 2 and up to 15 years were all separated into their own areas of the workhouse. From there on they were not supposed to communicate with each other. They 'shall respectively remain in the apartment assigned to them, without communication with any other class or subdivision of a class.'

There was a clause in the rules that allowed parents of children under 2 years, if they were 'desirous', to arrange to 'have an interview with such child at some time in each day, in some room in the workhouse to be appointed for that purpose'.

The discipline and diet were equally harsh. The minimum of food was provided twice a day – breakfast and dinner. Breakfast consisted of stirabout made from oatmeal or a mixture of Indian meal, oatmeal, rice and buttermilk. Depending on the finances of the Board of Guardians, the stirabout had higher levels of rice and less of the oatmeal and Indian meal. Dinner, in the middle of the day, was meant to consist of potatoes and buttermilk but with the potato scarcity from 1846 onwards was sometimes a

Workhouse interior 1845,
London Illustrated News.

thin meat and oatmeal soup or brown bread. If a supper was given it was bread and milk.

Each workhouse conformed to a standard day. Inmates were called to rise at 6 a.m. with breakfast soon after. Work took place until a meagre dinner at 12 p.m. and then back to work again until 6 p.m. Supper, if served, was between 6.30 and 7 p.m. and then it was straight to bed at 8 p.m. Once a week the inmates were washed and the men shaved.

Able-bodied men were expected to work in the fields, women in the preparation of food, laundry and general housework. Boys and girls under the age of 15 in theory attended classes but these were spasmodic and, due to the numbers (what is now called the teacher/pupil ratio), they were unmanageable for any teacher. On 9 October 1851 the master of Listowel Workhouse reported that the Bedford schoolmaster requested an assistant 'as it is impossible for one person to pay proper attention to 466 children in one class; all boys'.[5]

The Minutes of the Board of Guardians in Listowel also noted in their report on 12 September 1849:

> The Master begs to report that the education of the female children appears to be very much neglected at the Workhouse school. On yesterday when the Emigration Officer examined the girls, many of whom have been 2 years or more at this school, very few could even read very imperfectly. Only one or two make any attempt at writing.

The emigration officer requested the Matron to bring this matter under the serious attention of the Vice-Guardians. However, the Vice-Guardians, having discussed the matter, decided not to remove Miss Nolan, the teacher, 'in consideration of her excellent moral character' but it was not the first time that they had 'endeavoured to stimulate her to more energetic discharge of her duties'.

James Hack Tuke, a Quaker from York, England visited Ireland on a fact-finding mission and in the autumn/winter of 1847–48. He visited many workhouses, particularly in Connacht and in his report wrote 'Nearly two thirds of the inmates of Union houses of Connaught are, as may be expected, children, many of them orphans.' He was shocked by the neglected condition of the children. He stated:

> In many Unions, due to their bankrupt state, there are no books and no means whatever for providing the necessary books or school requisites; and thus we see hundreds of children wholly idle and unemployed where a few pounds expense would enable them to be taught.[6]

Articles 31, 32 and 33 dealt with religious rules. They were principally included in an effort to keep warring religious factions in line. Article 31 dealt with ministers of any religious persuasion who went into the workhouse to give religious assistance or instruct children. They were strictly 'confined to inmates who are of the religious persuasion of such minister, and to the children of such inmates'. Under Articles 32 and 33 it was allowed that 'inmates of 15 years and upwards, being of sound mind' could change the denomination of the religion which had originally been entered on the register. To counterbalance this, the minister involved in a change of religious persuasion of an inmate had to report the matter to the Master of the Workhouse, who in turn would report to the Board of Guardians and they would take the final decision. There was obviously good reason for these three articles, and indeed in each of the Kerry workhouses, we have incidents where inmates were accused of changing their religion for several different reasons and of ministers of both Roman Catholic and Established Church accusing each other of proselytising.

As the Famine continued in Kerry, all of the workhouses suffered from severe overcrowding. The numbers within the workhouses rose dramatically, auxiliary workhouses were opened in each of the towns to cope with the huge numbers of destitute arriving on a daily basis. This overcrowding gave rise to unhygienic conditions, leading to disease, and it was these diseases that in the main were responsible for the high death rates both in the workhouses and later in the fever hospitals. Lying in close proximity at night on planks covered with straw mattresses and a few rags, with very little ventilation, the only toilet facilities were covered cesspits.

The overcrowding and lack of basic hygiene was a recipe for disaster. Prevalent in the population already were the usual cases of tuberculosis, diarrhoea, flu and chest complaints from the damp environment. Added to those now came typhus, dysentery, smallpox, relapsing fever and cholera. The very young and the very old, already in a state of malnutrition, were unable to put up any resistance. The arrival of fever on the heels of the potato famine had another detrimental effect on the population. The 'black fever', as typhus was called, as it blackened the skin, was spread by body lice and was carried from location to location by beggars and homeless people. Together with tuberculosis it engendered such fear and superstition into families that normally kind and hospitable people shied away from their neighbours and became unsympathetic and unwelcoming. Some of those who were struck down by fever in their cabins were left to die and in a number of cases, relief workers who were exposed to the diseases succumbed themselves and died.

In Kerry, a number of priests died as a result of contracting famine-related diseases, some caught in the squalid conditions of workhouse ministering. Fr John Gallivan, Ballyferriter, Revd Michael Devine PP, Dingle, Fr Thomas Enright, Tralee, Fr Patrick Tuohy, Castlemaine, Fr Jeremiah Falvey, PP, Glenflesk, Fr John Donoghue PP, Kilgarvan all perished.[7] The Presentation and Mercy nuns, not long arrived in Kerry, were soon working in the great effort at providing some sustenance for their pupils, rather than teaching and educating as they had planned. The nuns in Listowel started with thirteen children, feeding them with breakfasts – bread, a mug of boiled rice and milk. 'During 1847 alone, the nuns in Listowel distributed 31,000 breakfasts to their starving female pupils.'[8] In Killarney the nuns set up a hospital in the partly finished Catholic cathedral and visited the fever-stricken in the crowded lanes, sometimes to coffin the dead.[9] In Dingle the nuns turned their school into a part hospital, part cook-shop. All this work brought great danger to the nuns themselves and resulted in numbers of them catching fever and some dying.

Entire families who did not get as far as the workhouse or fever hospital, devastated by hunger, sickness and weakness, simply laid down in their cabins or on the roadside and died. Those who died in their cabins remained among the living for days as their families were themselves too weak to move the bodies.

Hunger was one thing, but it could be combated, tackled and efforts made to alleviate it to some extent. Fever, however, threw up an almost impossible challenge. The continued poor hygiene, open drains, families living together in large numbers in substandard housing and no effective medicines all contributed to its spread.

Fr John Sullivan, parish priest of Kenmare, reported that on more than one occasion he visited houses where the corpses of father, mother and sometimes up to seven children lay side by side on a bed of straw.[10] Fr Sullivan was a tireless and active defender of his community. He kept up a continuous correspondence outlining the destitution, misery and desolation of his people with everyone from the Lord Lieutenant, and Sir Charles Trevelyan, Secretary of the Treasury to Earl Grey himself. He wrote on the 30 April 1849 to Sir William Sommerville, Chief Secretary for Ireland, at Westminster:

> Kenmare Workhouse ... Built originally for 500 paupers and therein was congregated for a considerable time, not less than 2400 paupers. The treatment the poor people received therein was enough to horrify the most hardened ... women raised out of bed at before 5 o'clock in the morning, three hours before day, after getting 7ozs of meal made into stirabout with a finish of sugar on it, they are bundled off again to try and keep some warmth.[11]

A report in the *Kerry Evening Post* of 10 March 1947 records:

> At Kilquane, a parish to the west of Dingle, one fifth of the inhabitants have already fallen victims to famine and disease. On Monday last, the decomposed remains of a father and his three children who had laid dead for eight days, were conveyed in baskets to be buried.[12]

From 1847 onward the Poor Law made landlords liable to pay rates for any tenant with land worth £4 or less. Landlords and their agents reacted in different ways. A number saw this as a heaven-sent opportunity to get rid of troublesome non-paying tenants. Others were more benevolent and lowered their rents or tried to provide employment, but these would have been in the minority. Many of the landlords just summarily evicted tenants to lower the taxes that they themselves would have to pay, leaving the tenant with no other option but to emigrate, if they could afford the fare, or alternatively take themselves and their family into the nearest workhouse for shelter. While tenants protested, 'any protests that now occur [were] the desperate expressions of a people literally maddened by hunger, disease and fear of death'.[13] According to the court and constabulary records, possibly as many as 45,000 families and 250,000 family members lost their homes and land in Munster and were put out on the road in the hungry years between 1846 and 1852.[14] Numbers of these evicted families added to the crowds trying to gain access to food and shelter in the workhouses.

Having gained admittance to the workhouse, there were very few ways out. Death was the main exit from this wretched place. Deaths were so numerous that corpses were carried on special carts day after day to be thrown into mass pauper graves or pits in specially set-up burial grounds either adjacent or in some cases within the workhouse grounds and covered in quicklime. Some had coffins which were specially constructed so that the bodies could be released into the graves directly and the coffin reused. The irony of this was that dying people got themselves admitted to the workhouse so that they would have a coffin and not be left to finish their lives on the side of the road or abandoned without a Christian burial. Traditionally there was a great respect for the dead, for the customary funeral wake and the customs and rites associated with a local death. These customs and rituals, which by necessity were abandoned during the Famine, became the norm again when that era was over.

Three of the workhouses in this study have a field nearby where hundreds of bodies were buried without names or any identification. These grounds are now titled Teampall Bán, 'God's Acre' and the roadways approaching them are usually titled Cosán na Marbh, 'Pathway of the Dead'.

According to Monsignor Padraig Ó Fiannachta of Dingle, some 5,000 people died in the Dingle Union during the Famine years. Many were buried in the graveyard which overlooks the town on the side of Cnoc a' Chairn, a short distance from the then workhouse, later the hospital.

In Kenmare the Old Kenmare Cemetery as it is now known is just out-side the town. The graveyard was the site of an early monastic settlement founded by St Finian of Innisfallen, who died at the end of the seventh century. The Church of St Finian is in now ruins. The Famine plot in this cemetery is also the resting place of upwards of 5,000 local people buried there between 1845 and 1852.

Aghadoe is the site of Killarney's Famine Graveyard. This was one of the few Unions where 'paupers' appear to have been deliberately buried away from the vicinity of the workhouse. The full tragedy of how many souls were buried under this hilly and picturesque ground may never be known.

In Listowel, with seven years of extreme hardship, initially the dead from the workhouse were buried in Gale Cemetary, a short distance outside the town on the Ballybunion road. We know from the Workhouse Minutes that approximately 2,000 were buried here, more than half of these were under the age of 15.[15] In February 1850, such were the numbers needing burial on a daily basis, a new purpose-built paupers' burial ground was opened a short distance from the workhouse, known locally as Teampall Bán. Between February 1850 and March 1852, 2,665 people were recorded on the Minutes as buried there. John Pierse, who has conducted significant research in this area, says that this number recorded may have been mini-mised by workhouse management and the Guardians, as it would indicate failure of the system and point out to the paupers' justification for their fear and detestation of the workhouse.[16]

By early 1848 some of the 'orphans' had been in the Kenmare, Killarney and Listowel workhouses since they opened on 1845. (In Dingle they would have been in the temporary workhouse since it opened there in February 1848.) Some of the girls were undoubtedly genuine orphans in that both parents were dead. Close family relationships then the norm would not have allowed these genuine 'orphan' children to be placed in the workhouse unless the family situation was desperate – it would have been a last resort. Others had been there only since the start of the Famine in 1846 or later and would have been a mix of those who had gone into the workhouse with the entire family or those who had one parent alive and who put a daughter in the workhouse to guarantee at least two meals a day and shelter.

A memory that has remained strong in Kerry folklore is the horror of the poorhouse. In the 1960s a teacher's threat to a reluctant student usually included a reference to 'ending up in the workhouse' if more effort was not put into studying. The stigma of having a 'workhouse' background remained with those who entered it and served to terrify those who managed to survive these hungry and disease-ridden times.

Catherine Ryan

Catherine Ryan was baptised on 6 June 1830 in Ballylongford Roman Catholic Church with an address as Tarbert, County Kerry. Her parents are listed as Michael Ryan and Margaret Driscoll. Records from Ballylongford Parish Register show that Catherine had two brothers, an older one called Patrick, born in 1829, and a younger one, Thomas, born in 1832.

Viv Melville, Catherine Ryan's great-great-great-granddaughter, continues:

Tarbert is a small town in the north of County Kerry, on the Shannon estuary. From Baptismal records it would appear that at the time of her birth, the family were living between Tarbert and Ballylongford, eking out a subsistence living on a small plot of rented farmland. In the 1832 Tithe Applotments record there is a Michael Ryan living at Carhoonakilla, Tarbert with 4 acres, 1 rood, 35 perches which would appear to be the Ryan family place. In Griffith's Valuation, (1848–1864) however, the same land is valued at only £4 5s. 0d. per year and no house is included. There is a house and land also in the name of Michael Ryan nearby, Cockhill townland valued at 11s and the Landlord there is William Sandes.[17] He was a member of the notorious Sandes lineage, but he has been described as 'the most fair-minded of the Sandes family.'

Catherine seems to have lost all her family during the Great Famine and she ended up in Listowel Workhouse.

Catherine was one of the lucky girls who travelled on the *Thomas Arbuthnot* with the humane Surgeon Superintendent Strutt looking after them. After arrival in Sydney and two weeks spent in the depot at Macquarie Street, Catherine had a Memo of Agreement with Henry G. Douglass, who was the physician for the Sydney Infirmary and Benevolent Asylum.

By April 1853, Catherine was in Melbourne, Victoria where she married Irishman Patrick Keays, in St Francis' RC Church. Patrick had come to Ireland from Queen's County, on board the ship *Lloyds* accompanied by his younger brother John. Patrick (26) is listed on the passenger register as a 'ploughman' and John (23) as a 'labourer'. They were listed as Roman Catholic and both could read and write. They had initially arrived in Sydney in 1850 but, like many, had been lured south by the gold discoveries in Victoria. On the shipping register Catherine was listed as being able to read and write, and yet she could only sign her marriage certificate in 1853 with an 'X'. It's possible she told a few 'white lies' to get herself accepted by the Earl Grey Scheme's commissioners. Letters written by her do survive but they were not written until 1914, suggesting that she learned to read and write in her later years.

After their marriage, Catherine and Patrick settled at Kangaroo Flat in the Bendigo goldfields, where they remained for much of the next twenty years and where Catherine spent most of her time producing a family of eleven children. In 1869, the Victorian government enacted the Free Selection Act in order to encourage the settlement of the mining population onto the farmlands of Victoria. Patrick and Catherine took up the offer in 1874 and applied for a lease of 320 acres at Tongala, 140 miles north of Melbourne, near the Murray River. Patrick was badly injured when logs fell on his legs, breaking one and badly crushing the other. Thinking he would never be able to work the land again, they were forced to give up the lease and returned to Golden Gully in Bendigo.

By 1877 however, Patrick had recovered sufficiently to apply for another land grant and by 1 June 1878, Catherine and Patrick began occupying a Crown Lease of 225 acres in the Parish of Narioka, near the town of Nathalia. This was harsh, dry land, which demanded unceasing efforts and deep reserves of courage and perseverance. Neither Catherine nor Patrick were young at this time – Catherine would have been about 48 and Patrick in his early 50s. Their eldest boys, William, Thomas, Michael and James, had all left home, but the family was still large: Margaret aged 20, Patrick 16, John 14, Joseph 11, Mary 9 and Peter the youngest at 5.

The first priority on acquiring land was shelter for their large family, so a slab hut was built comprising of two rooms with a bark roof. Optimistically they named their property 'Rosalind Park' after the beautiful park near their old home in Bendigo, and set about clearing and fencing the land. They gradually added a stable, barn, dairy and piggery and raised wheat, barley, cattle and pigs. But life was tough and Patrick's name appeared sometimes on the Arrears Lists when droughts, crop failures and loss of equipment and animals made it impossible to keep up with rent payments.

It seems that most of the Keays boys inherited their father's dream of striking gold. Having grown up on the goldfields, it was probably not surprising that 'life on the land' didn't initially appeal to them. All the boys except Thomas and Peter went seeking their fortunes in the goldfields of Queensland, Victoria, New South Wales or Western Australia. James Keays even ventured to South Africa, where he died in Durban of Madagascar Fever, aged 28. There were newspaper articles at the time, suggesting that James may have been involved with and even had been murdered by a fellow who was a contender for the Jack the Ripper title!

In the July of 1900, Catherine lost her husband of forty-seven years. Patrick was about 75 and died intestate. Catherine was appointed administrator of his estate and took over the running of his property, which at the time of Patrick's death, was valued at £1,411 5s 0d. The house had been expanded by this time and now consisted of a six-roomed weatherboard house with an iron roof. There was a detached slab kitchen also with an iron roof and several outbuildings including a stable, a blacksmith's shed and a dairy.

In January 1901, the lease of the property was transferred into Catherine's name and she became the official owner of Rosalind Park. Her youngest son Peter was the only one of her boys to remain on the property and he along with Catherine and his sister Margaret ran the property for the next twenty-one years. Peter married Cecelia Brown in 1910 but in 1913 she died giving birth to their daughter Mercia. So Catherine, at the age of 80, became the primary carer for her infant granddaughter. In letters to her son Tom in Melbourne, she spoke about having to use condensed milk because their cow was only giving enough for the baby, and mentioned that 'Mercia [was] beginning to creep and wants more attention'.

Catherine died at Rosalind Park on 7 August 1921 in her early nineties. She was a true pioneer, a woman of inspirational strength and endurance who had survived the Great Famine, the workhouse, a three-month voyage to an unknown land, twenty years on the goldfields, the births of eleven children and the deaths of three of them, and all the terrors and trials that the farming life in Australia could throw at her.

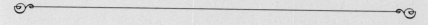

CIRCUMSTANCES
IN AUSTRALIA

HE EARL GREY Scheme was not the first scheme devised by the colonial authorities in conjunction with the British Government, in order to balance the male surplus then in existence in Australia. In 1831, a number of girls from an orphanage in Cork were sent to New South Wales, paid for by the colonial government. From this time onwards there were offers of free passage available to the colony for women emigrants. These efforts were not very successful, as at that time it was impossible to persuade women of 'good character' to travel alone on long sea voyages to an unknown and undeveloped land that had the reputation of being in the main a penal colony. As a result, the majority who travelled were women who had been taken off the streets of the main British cities – London, Liverpool and Dublin. While the authorities wanted and needed women to travel and successfully take up residence in Australia, no effort was made to look after them on the voyage or after their arrival. As a result, with no employment or accommodation arranged, many of these girls became prostitutes. In 1838, 600 homeless girls, the majority of them Irish, were wandering the streets of Sydney and sleeping out at night in the parks or beneath the shelter of rocks in area.

Following the end of convict transportation to Eastern Australia in August 1838, the colonial administrators had to consider how they would fill the labour workforce required to continue the expansion of their

Facsimile of The Colonist. *(Sydney, NSW: 1835–1840), 22 September 1840.*

the other. At present we find that great numbers of useless people are imported,—*prostitutes and vagabonds,* which occurs from the persons engaged in bringing them out being mere speculators, men who look at the profit and loss only.* A few respectable people are put on board, and then whole cargoes of people are sent by the steamboat *from the south of Ireland.*" If the honourable gentleman meant by this to insinuate that the present importers of Bounty immigrants are chargeable with a deliberate design in selecting "prostitutes and vagabonds" or "useless people," when they could get immigrants of a better sort, we have no hesitation in saying that the insinuation is a most unjust and unfounded one. The description of immigrants imported by the Government last year, and the prevalence of Irish among them, gave rise to numerous complaints, which did not pass unnoticed by the Committee; and it was then more than insinuated by the Press, that the Home Government were favouring Irish Emigration to this colony, in deference to the wishes and solicitations of O'CONNELL and his tail! These insinuations seem to have been indignantly spurned by Mr. ELLIOTT, the Emigration Agent General: for in one of his dispatches

developing colony. When looking for male labour, initially consideration was given to recruiting Chinese and Indians; £1,500 had been dispatched to Singapore that year with an 'order' for 100 such men.[1] This idea did not go very far, as the colonial authorities wanted white Europeans and in particular workers from what was regarded by most as 'the home country' – England. Understood, if not stated, was the expectation that these English workers would also espouse the Protestant faith and display a Protestant ethos of hard work and moral rectitude. In 1840, as the shortage of labour became acute, an Immigration Association was formed in South Australia, for the 'promotion and improvement of Bounty Immigration to this colony'.[2] While the aims of the association were admirable, the fact was that there was 'an urgent and increasing demand for labour' which was not being met by the Government to their satisfaction, and this was the driving force in the association. They were promoting the Bounty system to 'import 3550 adults of the best description', which they estimated would cost £71,000 [3] rather than the previous Government system. 'At present, we find that great numbers of useless people are imported – prostitutes and vagabonds ... a few respectable people are put on board and then whole cargoes of people are sent by the steamboat from the south of Ireland'.[4]

Initially efforts were made through the English Parliament and through newspapers there to try and 'sell' Australia as a desirable place to emigrate to, stressing the opportunities available there for people willing to work. However, it was a hard sell, with the prevalent view of the country as primarily a penal settlement.

At this particular time, Caroline Chisholm came to the fore. Mrs Chisholm was born in England, the daughter of a well-to-do farmer, and had been reared in the tradition of evangelical philanthropy.[5] She married, at 22, Captain Archibold Chisholm, a Catholic, and she later converted to Catholicism herself. Caroline accompanied her husband to India initially where he served in the East India Company. During their time there, they lived in Madras, where Caroline founded the Female School of Industry for the Daughters of European Soldiers. Following Captain Chisholm's posting to Sydney, Caroline immediately saw the problems facing the assisted female immigrants who remained in Sydney without employment or shelter and for whom the government had made no provision. Mrs Chisholm took it on herself to meet with the immigrant ships as they arrived; she found jobs for the girls and sheltered many of them in her own home. She lobbied Governor Gipps and Lady Gipps to provide a 'Female Emigrants' Home'. Despite discouragement and anti-Catholic feeling, she was eventually granted use of an old immigration barracks, keeping up to ninety women here at a time.

She then set out into the bush to the sheep and cattle stations with 'successive batches of Irish girls, placing them mainly as domestic servants in the homes of farmers of good character'.[6] By the time of her first report – *Female Immigration, Considered in a Brief Account of the Sydney Immigrants' Home* (Sydney, 1842) – she was able to announce the closure of the Female Emigrants' Home, as her policy for distributing female immigrants into the country areas had been so successful.[7] While there was still distrust of her motives and some criticism, the *Australasian Chronicle*, of Tuesday 12 August 1842 had to admit 'the value of Mrs Chisholm's philanthropic exertions, to which it is impossible to assign too much praise'.[8]

On the other side of the coin was John Dunmore Lang, a Presbyterian minister who had arrived in Sydney from Scotland in 1823. From his earliest days in New South Wales, Lang was a divisive and troublesome figure who made immediate enemies of both Anglicans and Catholics. He achieved initial notoriety by fighting with the governor Sir Ralph Darling over the provision of a dedicated Presbyterian college in the capital. On a visit back to England in 1830, he persuaded the Colonial Office to advance £3,500 for the establishment of a college in Sydney and to improve what he saw as the low moral tone of Australian society. He recruited and arranged for 140 Scottish workers and their families to emigrate to New South Wales. He arranged with them to repay their fares over a period, once they had started working. Lang was a bigoted but able leader of his flock. He established three newspapers in Australia, which were published up to 1851 and which he used to publicise his views and condemn those whom he saw as his enemies. 'He attacked fancy dress balls, Sabbath picnicking and alcoholic intemperance'.[9] He saw the colony as a dissolute, debauched place, filled with sexual and alcoholic immorality, and he blamed convict transportation for this. It didn't take him long to associate most of the convict transportation with Irish convicts. While Lang was not the only critic of the Irish he was one of the loudest. The *Sydney Morning Herald* took a powerful and bitter anti-convict stance and in that stand they laid most of the censure on Irish convicts rather than English. An example of this extreme racist attitude was evident in an article in *The Australian* on the 13 April 1846 when 'rating' the merits of labourers, placing a lowland Scotch or English labourer as equal to 'seven Irish or highlanders and to ten coolies'.

With the colonisation of the interior new areas were opening up all the time, leading to the demand for more immigrants, but by this time there was an increasing emphasis on females. While there was an urgent need for more labourers, farmhands and shepherds in the bush, there was also rapid development in the new urban settlements of Port Philip (Melbourne), South Australia (Adelaide) as well as Sydney in New South Wales. It was reckoned that by 1841, 80 per cent of the interior was populated by males. This situation had led, in aboriginal areas, to white men and 'gin women' cohabiting freely. Indeed we have an example of this in the epic story *Kings in Grass Castles*[10] in which Dame Mary Durack tells of her pioneering Irish family who built a cattle empire in Western Australia. Drovers, cattle and sheep herders who lived out in isolated areas of the bush for months on end were 'glad enough of the dusky companions whose only terms were the right to live and to serve'.[11]

Mixed-race babies resulting from these liaisons were regarded with hostility, often leading to abandonment and/or killing and in a later generation to the 'Stolen Children' experience. Religious and civil leaders came to the conclusion that the only solution to the problem was the introduction through immigration of a large supply of white women. This immigration initiative would solve two problems for the colonial administration. The women would initially be servants to the up and coming city bourgeoisie and to the country landowners who had been granted vast properties and who needed women to cook for their families and workers, to milk, feed farm animals, look after dairying and to mind their children. If these women were single they would then also be available for marriage to settlers, some free settlers and also a growing number of Ticket of Leave men who had served their sentences and were no longer looked down on as convicts.

Mrs Chisholm, with her husband, was back in England in 1847 and in giving evidence before a British Parliamentary Committee explained that, from her own experience, there was a pressing necessity not just to remedy the labour shortage in the colony but also an urgent need for women who would marry settlers. Armed with hundreds of petitions from New South Wales settlers, she demonstrated the need for both wives and workers. She also lobbied for reform of migration policy, including shipboard conditions for migrants. With her previous experience of settling girls by shrewd placement and by dispersing them individually to the outback, she recommended a similar approach to the reception of all female immigrants. However, she did not mention workhouses or indeed orphanages in this regard. John Dunmore Lang immediately responded with sectarian attacks on Mrs Chisholm, accusing her of promoting 'Popery' in the colony.

Mary Kennedy

Mary Kennedy was in Dingle Workhouse when she was selected to travel on the Earl Grey Scheme to Australia. On arrival, she declared her age as 17, her religion as Roman Catholic, and that her parents were Daniel and Debby (father living in Dingle, Kerry). Her descendants believe that Mary was baptised in Aunascaul on 28 February 1833 and her parents were Daniel Kennedy and Gobnet Keller [sic]. Mary would have had Irish as her first and possibly only language.

Ian Mac Andrews, great-great-grandson of Mary, takes up the story:

Mary left with the other Dingle girls from Plymouth on the *Thomas Arbuthnot* on 28 October 1849 and arrived in Port Jackson on 3 February 1850. Mary was also one of the luckier 'orphan' emigrants, in that her voyage with the other girls from Dingle, Listowel, Ennis, Galway, Loughrea, Ennistymon, Dublin and Scariff was overseen by the humane and caring Surgeon Superintendent Charles Strutt. On arrival, after spending some weeks in the depot in Sydney, she was sent onwards, travelling on the *Eagle* to Moreton Bay. Mary was initially indentured with James Cook of Ipswich and was employed later as a housemaid by John McIntyre of Ipswich, a storekeeper, at £6–£8 per year. Two years later, on 28 July 1853, she married William Samuels at Drayton Parsonage, Aubingy, then part of New South Wales, now in the State of Queensland.

I believe that Mary & William must have been some of the original settlers on the Darling Downs in Queensland at Drayton Swamp based on the fact that Mary was a Roman Catholic but they were married in the Drayton Parsonage (Church of England) as there was no RC church at that time & not even a Church of England church, just a parsonage. Both Mary and William signed the marriage certificate with an X.

William Samuels went to work for William Horton, who had arrived in Australia in 1832 as a convicted felon. Horton had been transported

---

Obituary of William Samuels husband of Mary Kennedy per *Thomas Arbuthnot* from *The Toowoomba Chronicle* 9 March 1893.
Mr William Samuels, a very old identity of Drayton, died at the Toowoomba Hospital on Tuesday morning at the ripe age of 73 years. Forty years ago he was familiarly known as "Horton's Sam," and was one of the best teamsters on the Ipswich road before the era of the railways. He piloted in his day thousands of bales of Eton Vale wool to Ipswich, and returned to Drayton with hundreds of tons of goods for the late Mr William Horton, who regarded Mr Samuels as one of the most trustworthy carriers on the road. The old Drayton identities are one by one joining the "silent majority," and the death of Mr Samuels removes another from the rapidly diminishing number. A large family are left to mourn the loss of a good father and a devoted husband. The funeral took place yesterday afternoon, and many old friends and residents followed the remains to the grave.

Funeral notice of Mrs Wm Samuels (Mary Kennedy) *Toowoomba Chronicle* 4 January 1902
It is again our regretful duty to record the death of an old resident of the district—Mrs William Samuels, who passed over at the Hospital on Wednesday at the age of 67 years. Death was due to the effects of a blood vessel bursting, and paralysis on one side. The late Mrs Samuels left her native county in Ireland at the age of 17, and after spending some time at Ipswich, at which place she was married, she came to Drayton with her husband—that place being then the principal town of the Downs. Between Drayton and Eton Vale she has resided ever since. Deceased, who was generally respected, leaves a family of nine (living) all married, and to them we tender our sincere condolences. The funeral took place yesterday afternoon.

The obituary and funeral notice of Mary and William Samuels, Queenslander, *18 March 1893.*

for stealing a coat. A free man from 1839, he worked initially as a stockman which took him north from the Hunter Valley in 1840 to a station at the Severn River, just south of the Queensland border. Here, Horton met early pastoralists including those who were the first to explore the Darling Downs. He was later at publican and businessman in Drayton, building the Royal Bull's Head Inn there in 1847. The slab-built inn with shingled roof, served as an important meeting place for the squatters.

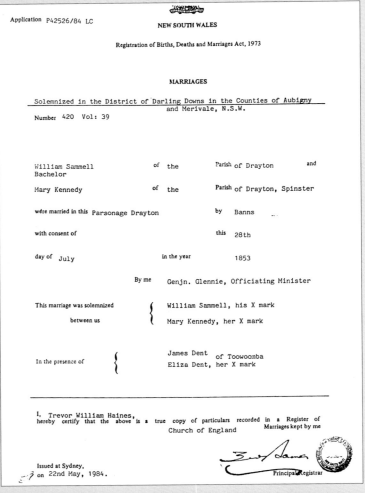

The marriage of Mary Kennedy and William Samuels, Drayton, 28 July 1853.

The inn was large and well equipped with a parlour and all the requirements for a constant stream of visitors, including travellers, clergymen, settlers and anyone travelling to the area from the coast.

In 1848 the Revd Benjamin Glennie conducted the first Church of England service on the Darling Downs at the Royal Bull's Head Inn and it was this clergyman who married Mary and William in 1853. 'Glennie's parish was the whole of the Moreton Bay (Brisbane) and the Darling Downs. According to his first Australian Diary, he travelled 1300 hundred miles in one year.'[12]

From this time on the Samuels family lived at Drayton and we know from William's obituary that he worked as a teamster on the Ipswich road, before the era of the railways, for Samuel Horton, taking wool to Ipswich and returning with much needed supplies for the ever-expanding number of Queensland settlers and squatters. These pioneer squatters and settlers were exposed to dangers and hardship that William and Mary would have shared in. Over the next twenty-one years, Mary had twelve children and only one of these appears to have died in infancy. This was an almost miraculous occurrence in an era of such extreme living conditions. Mary would have had complete responsibility for rearing, feeding and educating her large family while William was on the road. It would have been a lonely existence without schools, doctors or churches. She would have had to nurse her sick children herself, help other women to do the same, combat the heat, dust, drought and dangerous wildlife, together with the normal daily back breaking work.

Mary outlived William by nine years and died when she was sixty-nine years old. Nine of her children survived her; Sarah (d. 1861), Ellen (d. 1866) and William (d. 1896) were dead by this time.

In Australia, the newly arrived governor of New South Wales, Sir Charles Augustus Fitzroy, set to rectifying the situation. Governor Robe of South Australia suggested that part of the South Australian Land Fund be used to attract emigrants. Sir Daniel Copper, the Speaker of the New South Wales Legislature, also wrote to Thomas Spring-Rice, Lord Monteagle, the Irish Peer, 'We wish to receive emigrants; we are willing to pay for them. There are millions among you dying of hunger, let us have those starving crowds; here they will find a superabundance of the necessaries of life.'[13]

In Ireland, the extent of the Famine from 1845 onwards, with hundreds arriving daily to the workhouse doors, was putting extreme pressure on the individual Boards of Guardians to provide food and shelter for the rapidly growing numbers of these destitute families. Children usually made up about half of the workhouse population. These children and young people were either orphans whose parents had died, or who had been left at the workhouse by one parent unable to provide and who would have intended to return for them at a future date. Public funds and local taxes were being exhausted by the level of expenditure required to keep the system afloat. Furthermore, there was very little possibility of any of these young people getting work, enabling them to leave the workhouse, and this applied in particular to the girls.

On 16 March 1848 the 'Right Honourable Earl Grey', Secretary of State for the Colonies, received a despatch from Sir C.A. Fitzroy, sent in September 1847 urging a renewal of emigration and enclosing a copy of a report from the Colonial Government showing that 'a supply of labour is indpensably [sic] necessary for its prosperity'.[14] A theme running through the request to the British Parliament was the problem of a lack of labour affecting both sheep and cattle production and the cost of such labour, both of which would have an undue bearing on the success or otherwise of the development of the colony. The report included Minutes from a Select Committee which pointed out, among other things, that while shepherds more than any other type of labour were required, also 'families residing in towns are greatly in want of domestic servants'.[15] Alexander Mollison of Mount Macedon, Port Philip stated: 'I know some families in Melbourne in which the ladies are doing their own domestic work.' In May 1847 the want of domestic servants was causing 'very great discomfort to many families'.

In all the above reports, colonial authorities refer to England as the 'Mother Country', thereby reminding the imperial powers of their loyalty and the immeasurable possibilities of developing this huge continent with its attending prospect for joint prosperity.

At the same time as the 'lack of domestic servants' was causing 'very great discomfort' in Melbourne, in Westminster, the Select Committee on Poor Laws (Ireland), Third Report, was examining all of the problems being thrown up by the Famine – poverty, destitution, evictions, emigration and the overcrowding of workhouses. Edward Senior, Assistant Poor Law Commissioner, a committed and compassionate public servant, giving evidence at this Select Committee, stated that in his opinion it would be of the utmost importance to relieve the pressure on the workhouses by emigration. He went further by suggesting that those who would benefit most would be 'persons aged from 13 or 14 to 18 or 19, especially girls'.[16] He stated that the 'accumulation of young women in the workhouses is now much greater than young men'.[17] Mr Senior had already given a lot of thought to the desperate situation in the workhouses. He also suggested that respective Unions should defray the cost of clothing and removal to the port of embarkation, and that the Imperial Treasury or sale from the land fund of the colonies should be used to defray the remaining expenses. He stated that the emigration of these females would be advantageous in most of the Australian settlements, adding, 'I may explain that the tendency to a dead weight in the workhouses on the part of children is constantly increasing in every part of Ireland; epidemics and fevers and other causes, carry off the heads of the family, but the children are left; more than half of the inmates of the workhouses now consist of children.'[18]

By January 1848, Earl Grey, anxious to keep the colonists happy, informed Fitzroy that the Commissioners of Colonial Land and Emigration had taken steps to renew emigration to Australia. He explained that due to 'abundance of employment in Great Britain' and consequent lack of emigrants from there, it would be necessary fill the void from Ireland. 'They also have taken steps, as you will perceive, designed to admit of sending out a larger proportion than heretofore of single women.'[19]

By February 1848, Grey was more specific. He informed Fitzroy that in order to keep up the supply of labour, 'a free passage to New South Wales should be offered to certain classes of orphans of both sexes in Ireland between the ages of 14 and 18.'[20] 'Although I have not yet received any official communication of the assent of the Irish Government to the conditions of the proposal, I have no reason to doubt that it will be given'.[21]

He also outlined the conditions that should prevail both on the voyage and in Australia for these young persons. Only 'responsible persons' who were in a position to offer instruction in the occupations 'which will be most useful to them' should be considered as potential employers. They should be placed 'within reach of the superintendence of some clergy-man of their own religion, and the proposed Committee in Australia were to act as guardians in cases of masters failing to discharge their duties.

By March 1848 a scheme had been worked out with the Irish Poor Law Commissioners. 'It involved the selection of young orphan females between 14 and 18 years of age who would be sent as emigrants to the Australian colonies, where, it was hoped they would in time become the wives of settlers.'[22] It is not surprising that Grey should find this a suitable solution to the pressing needs of further developing the Australian Colonies. In February 1847 there were 63,000 children among the workhouse population of 116,000; by the middle of 1849 the number had increased to 90,000.[23] The general situation in Ireland was difficult and looked like become a long-term problem.

Each Poor Law inspector received a letter dated 7 March 1848 from the Commissioners for administering the Laws of Relief of the Poor in Ireland (called the Commissioners) informing them of the decision and communications from Earl Grey explaining the manner in which the emigration of young females 'is proposed to be conducted'.[24] The Commissioners made it plain that they expected the Boards of Guardians to address themselves to the objective without delay. They were advised that the young persons are 'duly and properly apprised of prospects which await them in the event of their availing themselves of the free passage to Australia' and the final line of the letter pointed out the responsibility of the Boards to 'bear the cost of the outfits and the expense of conveyance to the place of embarkation'.[25]

The Commissioners and the colonial authorities were keen to avoid blunders that had been made in previous emigration efforts. While choosing the right sort of girl was to be the responsibility of the Emigration Inspector appointed, Lieutenant Henry and the individual Boards of Guardians in Ireland, the responsibility of getting respectable employers in Australia rested with the 'Orphan' Committees established in South Australia, Port Philip and New South Wales.

In outlining the scheme, the Emigration Commissioners placed great emphasis on this occasion of the importance of selecting only suitable candidates. The colonists wanted now to attract a more respectable immigrant rather than the convicts, paupers and other undesirables from Britain and Ireland that had been the mainstay of settlers for the previous forty years.[26]

At this point, the scheme met with satisfaction all round. The Australians would get females who would become 'active and useful members of society', the Boards of Guardians and Poor Law Commissioners would get some relief from the pressure on the workhouses and consequently on their funds, the British Government would be seen to be active and responsible. Although the British Treasury was not involved in this scheme, with his usual thoroughness, Charles Trevelyan attempted to impose his own views on it. A habitual controller, he insisted that the Emigration Commissioners should submit to him personally regular reports of their activities.

Honora Jones

Honora Jones was one of the Listowel orphans who travelled on the *Thomas Arbuthnot* and arrived in Port Jackson in 3 February 1850. Her arrival records tell us that she was 16 years of age, her parents, John and Ellen, were both dead and she was a Roman Catholic.

Honora does not have a descendant to tell her story; it has been left to an unknown 'lady since removed from the colony' to give us a description of what happened to Honora and seven members of the Thatcher family who perished in the Gundagai Floods of June 1852.[27]

These girls who journeyed into the interior in the company of Dr Strutt were the 'lucky girls', as they were treated with care and compassion by the doctor, both on the ship and later when he went to so much trouble to get 'good' placements for them. These Dingle and Listowel girls were no doubt more fortunate than any of the other orphans, but Honora's good luck ran out very quickly.

She was employed in late March 1850 by R.P. Jenkins, a substantial landowner at his property, Browenor at Bangus near Gundagai, at £8 per year, no doubt with the approval of Dr Strutt. Just a year and a half later, Honora married Henry Thomas Thatcher on 25 October 1851. At some point in the following months, Henry left for the 'diggings'. Like most other young men of the time, he visualised hitting it rich in the goldfields. He left his young wife in the care of his parents and family.

The original settlement of Gundagai was founded in 1838 at a crossing on the Murrumbidgee River. This particular crossing on the Sydney to Melbourne road had been identified by Captain Charles Sturt as a favourable place to cross the river. The town grew quickly but most of the development took place on the banks of the river or the adjacent river mudflats. A number of floods had occurred, but none like that which inundated the area in June 1852. Although the Aborigines gave the settlers warning about the threat of the coming floods and moved their camps to higher ground, nobody paid attention.

We have a contemporary account of the terrors of the flood written by this 'lady since removed from the colony' and published in the *Sydney Morning Herald* on 3 March 1855. She herself, her three-week-old baby, husband and three other children spent three days clinging to the roof of their bark hut in the middle of seas of churning water, until they were miraculously rescued by 'Jacky', their aboriginal neighbour. Having described how quickly the flood rose and their situation on the roof, she also gives us a picture of their neighbours, the Thatchers.

Having spent the first night on the roof, she goes on to tell us:

Day began to dawn, which cheered us very much. About 10 o'clock we saw a boat approaching us to our great joy; however, it passed us; my husband hailed them; there were four men in the boat; they answered us and said they would relieve us when they rescued a family farther on, who appeared in more danger than we were, their cottage being a weatherboard one, and situated much lower than our house; this family was a Mr. Thatcher's four sons and one daughter, 16 years of age; we saw them all enter the boat.

The lady goes on to explain that the boatmen would not take Mr Thatcher, Mrs Thatcher or Mrs Thatcher junior (Honora) as the boat was full with five children and the four oarsmen. They left Mr and Mrs Thatcher and Honora still clinging to their roof, with the promise that they would return for them. The stream they were trying to row in:

> appeared to get more furious and the boat was thrown from side to side, crashing into logs and debris floating by.
>
> Anxiously did we watch them; they had just got in the middle of the river, the boat struck with fearful force on an immense tree. We saw the boat spring out of the water, and fall again, head first and sink in an instant. The burst of grief from the now bereaved parents, may be better imagined than expressed, it was heart-rending in the extreme. Such a scene I never before witnessed, and trust that I may never again.
>
> Poor Mrs. Thatcher Jnr., was in a sad state, her husband, a very worthy young man, was absent at the diggings; he left his young wife with his father and mother during his absence. I distinctly heard her several times call her husband by name, 'Henry, oh Henry, could I but see you for one moment, I would die happy'. Her piteous lamentations we heard up to the moment she perished. Mrs. Thatcher senior, sat with her baby, her hands clasped after the first burst of grief was over, she uttered not a word.

It was now Friday night. With darkness approaching, both families had been on the roofs of their houses for over twenty-four hours.

> Between eight and nine o'clock, crash went Mr. T's cottage, they were on the roof, but were soon out of sight; the roof broke, Mr. Thatcher grasped a tree, his wife, child and daughter-in-law, were swept from his side in an instant and perished. He remained in that tree until Sunday noon when he was taken off by Jacky, an Aboriginal.

The 'lady' and her family were eventually rescued by the same Jacky. The Aboriginal's boats were made of bark and more navigable on the raging waters. She continues to relate what happened afterwards, which is why she is now 'late of this colony'. On being rescued, there were hundreds of people gathered on shore to meet and help those who survived. There were 'bursts of rejoicing … tears of joy were shed by men that doubtless had not done so for many years before'. At least eighty-nine people had perished in the floods, which still holds the record for the worst flood in Australian history. Gundagai was now a desolate waste and while there was excitement for many months after the flood, plunder started almost right away, in a 'barefaced manner'. Both the actual inhabitants and people on their way through to the diggings started to help themselves to all the possessions that had floated out of the small cottages. The 'lady' saw several of her own dresses on other women and children wearing her daughter's dresses 'while mine were destitute of a change of clothing'.

This convinced the family to leave the colony – 'I did not leave it without bitter feelings of regret. It was the home of my childhood'.

Honora is remembered on the Gundagai Flood Plaque.

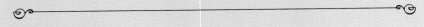

~4~

WORKHOUSE
DECISIONS

THE EARL GREY Scheme was met with differing reactions in Ireland. Most of the Poor Law Unions welcomed the proposals as a solution to the problems of overcrowding and associated costs of keeping the orphans indefinitely. Almost half of the inmates of the workhouses were children under the age of 15, either genuinely orphaned or abandoned temporarily by their parents in the hopes that they would survive.

In Kerry, Guardians of four of the six workhouses – Dingle, Kenmare, Killarney and Listowel – decided to participate. However, Tralee Union turned down the scheme. Cahirciveen did not take part either. The Guardians in Tralee were not impressed. Two of those present at the meeting when the matter was proposed, objected to it on principle, saying that 'the emigration of the bone and sinew of the country should not be encouraged'.[1] Other Tralee Guardians based their objections on the precarious state of the Union's finances.[2] They were prescient in this view, as shall be seen later, in that a number of the neighbouring Unions had problems paying for the outgoings they would be responsible for, due to their continuous cash-flow difficulties. While the Australian Government was picking up the costs of transportation from Plymouth to the colony, the Unions would be expected to outfit the girls with clothing and shoes, and they would also be responsible for the costs of conveying them firstly from Kerry to either Dublin or Cork and by steamer thence to Plymouth.

The quarterdeck of an emigrant ship at Plymouth, 1850.

Emigrant Ship, Illustrated London News, 1850.

Many others in the country were not in favour, in particular nationalist newspapers. Then, as now, there was ambivalence in Ireland towards emigration. Those with a nationalist viewpoint saw it as detrimental. For them the simple fact that the English Parliament had suggested and sanctioned the scheme meant that it could not be beneficial to Ireland. *The Nation* labelled the scheme as 'one of the most diabolical proposals ever made or conceived since Cromwell's time'.[3] The *Tipperary Vindicator* called the proposal a form of white slave traffic.[4] In Kenmare, the respected parish priest Fr John Sullivan disapproved of the scheme, as he did later of the Landsdowne Estate assisted emigration scheme to migrate 3,500 'paupers' from these estates to America. His attitude to any emigration was that it would be 'the active, the healthy and the industrious' who would go while 'the drones would be left behind'.[5]

In all, 117 girls aged from 14 to 20 years old left Kerry between 28 October 1849 and 8 April 1850 from workhouses in Dingle (20), Kenmare (25), Killarney (35) and Listowel (37). We have no idea of the views or attitudes of the orphans themselves to their proposed emigration to Australia. The Emigration Commissioners, when deciding to send only females, also stressed that the scheme was to be voluntary. It is not certain how many of the girls volunteered totally of their own accord or if there was an element of being pushed to go. Maybe it was only those with the courage to go, echoing Fr Sullivan's view that it would be 'the active, the healthy and the industrious' who could see a brighter future ahead. We will see from the later lives of those who went, that in the main they had all these attributes allied to strong survival instincts.

With a very poor educational background – some were unable to read or write, and in the main they spoke Irish as their first tongue – the girls who were selected for the Earl Grey Scheme were being offered a leap into the unknown. Australia as a destination would have been beyond their limited imagination. They would have little or no concept of where it was, what their lives there would be like or importantly how far away it was from their communities in Kerry. While some of them were genuine orphans with no known kith or kin, at least half of the Kerry orphans had one or more parent and perhaps sisters or brothers living either in the workhouse or in the locality.

Did they realise that they would never again see their families? Emigration at this time was for life. Did they understand that after arrival, they could be separated from their workhouse companions by huge distances? Even with these unknowns ahead of them, the evidence we have is that considerable numbers of girls within the workhouses were anxious to be 'selected'. One has to assume that most of the girls saw an opportunity that was worth taking, a way of leaving the miserable conditions in the dreaded poorhouse, no matter what the future would bring.

One of the biggest challenges facing the Poor Law Commissioners in 1848 was how to cope with the huge numbers arriving at the workhouses. Females would have a very poor chance of ever being discharged from the workhouse as there was little or no employment available for them. Neither were there apprenticeships available for females. Their 'workhouse' status would militate against them ever getting whatever paid work might become obtainable. Once they entered the workhouse they were regarded as inferior beings, and if they had been there for a number of years they became institutionalised and were regarded as difficult and troublesome. This was another reason for the Guardians to encourage volunteers to the scheme and to move them on at a young age.

The rules adopted by the Poor Law Commissioners[6] for the selection of 'suitable applicants' included that the orphans should be between the ages of 14 and 18, be of 'industrious habits and good character', free from all disease and vaccinated against smallpox. It was important that they should be unmarried so that there would be no impediments to marrying Australian settlers. They were also required to have a sufficient knowledge of reading, writing and arithmetic, and the principles of the Christian religion. An 'orphan' was defined as having lost at least one parent to death or abandonment. In order to prevent people from entering the workhouse for the sole purpose of obtaining assisted migration, the offer was limited to those who had previously been resident in the workhouse for at least one year.

The records we have from the Board of Guardian Minutes are excellent from some Unions and poor from others. Records had to be returned to the Poor Law Commissioners in Dublin on a weekly basis to a set format. They were mostly concerned with finances, the weekly costs incurred, the rates collected or not, the ordering of supplies of food and reports from the Master and officers, the medical doctor and, importantly, 'orders from the Poor Law Commissioners'. There was also a weekly sheet to be filled in giving the numbers in the workhouse, the numbers receiving outdoor relief, the number that had entered, and the numbers that had been born, discharged and/or had died. There are no documents surviving showing names of inmates admitted or those who died or left.

All of the Unions recorded the correspondence received from the Poor Law Commissioners in Dublin, dated 7 March 1848, forwarding to them several copies of a communication made to Earl Grey by the Colonial Land and Emigration Commissioners on the subject of 'young persons at present inmates of Irish workhouses who may be eligible for emigration to South Australia'. The Commissioners were 'most anxious that advantage should be taken of this proposal of the Government'. They also reminded the Unions that 'you will ascertain from the Board of Guardians, distinctly, their willingness to bear the cost of outfit and the expense of conveyance to the place of embarkation'.[7]

Killarney

Just one month after receiving the letter from the Poor Law Commissioners, on 29 April 1848 the Minutes of the Killarney Board of Guardians record:

It was resolved 'that in reference to the Letter of the Commissioners of Colonial Lands and Emigration to the Under Secretary for the Colonial

Department ... the Master having reported after due inquiry that there are about 150 Paupers in the House of the age of 14 to 18 years willing to emigrate to the Colonies this Board beg to call the attention of the Poor Law Commissioners to this Report.'

Furthermore, it was resolved 'that this Board are willing to convey such persons as shall be selected for emigration to Plymouth at the expense of the Board and also to furnish them with such outfit as the Commissioners require in the Memorandum attached to the letter of the 17th February'.[8]

It is no great surprise that '150 Paupers' were willing to emigrate when the numbers of women in the workhouse that week comprised 371 girls (aged 9 to 15 years) and 261 'able bodied females' with a total complement of 1259 inmates including children. The Board was also responsible for 346 patients in the fever hospital.

However, matters in Killarney moved slowly after this. On 20 May 1848 while the Guardians were submitting their list to the board, they also enquired if it would be possible 'whether the Ships in which it is proposed to send out these orphans could call at Cork for them which arrangement would save the expense of sending them to Plymouth.' When this request was turned down, the clerk reported to the Guardians on 24 June 1848 'that Major Bolton attended at the Workhouse on Saturday 24 inst instant and inspected the female orphans returned on a list for Emigration to Australia by the Board of Guardians ...' Importantly the clerk also noted on these minutes that:

It was resolved that the Master having stated to this Board that there are at present in this Workhouse several young females between the ages of 14 and 18 years not Orphans but who in every other respect come within the regulation of the Emigration Commissioner's Letter of 17th February last most anxious to emigrate to Australia, this Board therefore request the Commissioners for administering the Laws for Relief of the Poor in Ireland to forward if in their power the desire which these young females have individually expressed and which is also that of their respective parents, including such of them as may on examination be found eligible for Emigration with those already selected by Major Bolton which this Board consider will tend to their future welfare and should the Commissioners accede to this request,

Minute Book, Killarney Board of Guardians, 29 April 1848. (Kerry Local History Library, Tralee)

this Board will supply the funds necessary to convey these young persons to Plymouth and also the Outfit required in the Memorandum attached to the above mentioned Letter of the 17th February.

The Killarney Board does not appear to have received permission for any more than thirty-five emigrants and there is no mention of the 'orphans' again until 28 January 1849 when we learn from the Minutes that the clerk had written to each of the Guardians of the Union to inform them that the Earl of Kenmare and Henry A. Herbert Esq. had offered 'a loan of money for the purpose of enabling the Board to carry out the provisions of the several Poor Law Acts for the Emigration and the subject will be brought forward for the consideration of the Board on Monday 3 February next.'[9] Like a number of other Unions at this time, the Killarney Union was undoubtedly suffering from cash problems and the actual arrangements for emigration of the orphans had become something of a challenge. The offer of a £2,000 loan from Lord Kenmare and Henry A. Herbert was turned down by the Board on the 13 February 1949.[10] We are not told what the reason for this decision was, but they had probably little prospect of repaying what would now equal around €20,000 and could possibly be surcharged personally if all the paperwork was not correct.

Fully one year after the first decision to accede to the request to send the orphans from Killarney, we finally learn from the Minute Book of the 2 May 1849 that the Commissioners in Dublin are complaining to the Board in Killarney:

> Adverting to the Commissioner's letter of 19th ult, relating to the Female Orphans' proposed as Emigrants to South Australia and stating that the Commissioners have not as yet received the names of the individuals selected but presume that a list of the names has been left at the workhouse by Lieut. Henry to whom any certificate of character required, but which may not already have been forwarded, should be sent and requesting that the Guardians will make the necessary arrangements without delay if not already made.[11]

The Killarney orphans finally left from Penrose Quay in Cork by a steam vessel for Plymouth on 24 May 1849. Mystery surrounds the 'list of names' of individuals selected, as mentioned in the Minutes on 2 May 1849 and previously on 20 May 1848, as neither copy exists in the appropriate Minute Book records. The loss of these records has serious consequences for the identification of the thirty-seven girls who emigrated from Killarney, as we shall see later.

Ellen Powell

Ellen Powell from Scrahane, Killarney was one of the unluckier girls, in that she travelled on the *Elgin* to Adelaide, arriving on 12 September 1849. These girls were not looked after very well by those charged to oversee their welfare, and as a result, some fell foul of the law in the following years.

The South Australian Register listed the full complement of passengers, including Government emigrants – a number of families and their children as well as 'female orphans'.[12]

Unfortunately, while we have a full list of the girls on the *Elgin*, neither their home places nor the workhouses that they originated from, have been recorded. Because of the diligence of two of Ellen's great-granddaughers – Gayle Dowling and Gabrielle Bartels – we have a record of Ellen's subsequent life in Australia.

Ellen was born to Catherine Flynn and John Powel (sic) in Scrahan, Killarney. Her parents were not married. Her father was not a Catholic and, unusually, allowed Ellen to have his family name when she was baptised 4 December 1826 in Killarney. He appears to have been an overseer or agent for Lord Kenmare, occupying land at Scrahan beside the Kenmare estate. There is no subsequent record of her mother Catherine Flynn marrying anyone else in the Kerry area, so she may have died before Ellen's departure for Australia. Her father would have been an influential man with the Killarney Board of Guardians and he may have arranged that she would be part of the group selected to emigrate. He was still alive in Killarney at this time. He is recorded in Griffith's Valuation of 1852 as occupying the land in question. The wider Powell family were well to-do in Killarney and the Castleisland area.

While we have no record of Ellen's apprenticeship or her time in South Australia, we know that by 1854 she had moved from South Australia and was established in Melbourne, Victoria, where on 7 January 1854 she married Richard Thomas Burke at St Francis Catholic Church.

Gayle and Gabrielle take up the story:

Ellen Powell's husband, Richard, was born around 1829 and came from Westmeath Ireland. The marriage certificate is ambiguous. It indicates that both Richard and Ellen had previous relationships resulting in children, by ticking off boxes but Ellen is declared as a spinster and Richard declared '–'. Whatever the case, the certificate suggests that the early years after stepping onto McLaren Wharf in Adelaide had not been easy for Ellen.

Richard Burke initially worked as a butcher in Little Bourke Street Melbourne. He and Ellen had one child in Richmond in 1855 before uprooting, moving inland and becoming a gold-mining family. There are children born in Ararat and Moonambel before the family eventually settled in Drummond, Victoria, also a mining area. Together they had nine children, with four dying in infancy.

In 1871 Richard is paying rates for a hut on Crown land in Drummond with seven residents. Ellen and Richard appear to have lived a modest life with their surviving children marrying Malmsbury-based families and twenty-two grandchildren to carry on their name.

Richard died first, on 18 October 1891 aged 62, followed by Ellen on 12 September 1899 aged 73. They are buried in the Malmsbury Cemetery with a headstone to mark their final resting places.

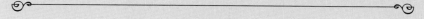

Listowel

Listowel, while not giving a lot of information on their correspondence with the Poor Law Commissioners, seemed to make their decision without controversy. Having received the letter from the Poor Law Commissioners outlining the Earl Grey Scheme in spring 1848, a decision had been made by the Guardians to adopt the scheme for the Listowel Union, and by September 1849 Lieutenant Henry RN had visited Listowel to choose and personally select suitable emigrants. We should remember that this decision was made in the light of the Guardians battling with crises on all sides on a weekly basis. Listowel Union was continually teetering on the verge of bankruptcy. In March 1849 the Minutes note that the manager of the Provincial Bank 'having declared under any circumstances to honour cheques on that Establishment beyond the actual amount of Cash to our credit ... are unable to meet our liabilities'.[13] The records of the Minute Books provide a vivid picture of the problems and struggles faced by the Union in the months of September and October. There were the usual complaints and problems; food stores being stolen, storekeepers sacked, rent collectors misappropriating the rents, milk and grain suppliers of an 'inferior' standard, 'disorderly paupers', dissension among the Board, and due to the huge numbers seeking admission, permission had to be sought from the commissioners in Dublin to open auxiliary workhouses. There were also issues with ratepayers complaining about the rates levied on them and their inability to pay.

In the case of Trinity College, who were the landlords of one-third of the area of the Union, it was recorded for the Commissioners in Dublin that 'destitution of this Union is mainly attributable to the insufficience [*sic*] of this tenure'.[14] While the Union would be taking on the initial costs of outfitting and conveying the orphans to Dublin, an opportunity to rid themselves of the ongoing costs of seventeen inmates would initially be more than welcome and provide much-needed space for the crowds still trying to gain admittance to the workhouse.

While Lieutenant Henry was highly regarded and punctilious in his duties, he selected them by 'walking through making his choice'[15] and while they were medically checked, did he take into account that a number of them could neither read nor write, that they had little or no practical training as housemaids or domestic servants and that at least in one case, one of those selected, had a mental disorder? Or alternatively, did he think that each of the girls selected would be suitable for training into these fields after their placement on arrival? We have no record of his thought process but it is evident that the criteria for selection appears to have been largely ignored and it was one of the major flaws that worked against the success of the scheme as all of these negative issues would affect their settlement in Australia.

And again, did the girls have a real choice – whether to go or stay? There were a number of 'push' factors from the girls' perspective. The 'poorhouse' as they called it, was a shameful experience, living conditions were extremely basic, they were ill-fed and ill-clothed. A number of them could neither read nor write, notwithstanding the 'schools' run in the workhouses. Indeed, following the inspection of Lieutenant Henry there was a report from the master to the Board at the following Listowel Meeting:

> The Master begs to report that the education of the female children appears
> to be very much neglected at the Workhouse school. On yesterday when the
> Emigration Officer examined the girls, many of whom have been 2 years or

more at this school, very few could even read very imperfectly. Only one or two make any attempt at writing.[16]

The Listowel girls, hailing from the Baronies of Iriaghticonnor and Clanmaurice, would have experienced friends and relations in the work-house being taken away for burial to Gale cemetery and later on to mass graves in Teampall Bán, on a daily basis, as a result of hunger, overcrowding and disease, so the prospect of a journey, any journey, out of the workhouse would have been better than remaining where they were.

The Minutes note that 'Lieutenant Henry (Emigration Officer) this day examined the several orphan girls in the Workhouse and selected the following for emigration to Australia'.[17]

Mary Brandon *Newtownsandes*	Johanna Hayes *Kiltomey*	Mary Purcell *Listowel*	Ellen Wilson *Listowel*
Ellen Casey *Ratoo*	Hanna Jones *Listowel*	Margaret Stack *Kiltomey*	Mary Wilson *Listowel*
Mary Casey *Duagh*	Eliza Moriarty *O'Dorney*	Catherine Ryan *Listowel*	Ellen Leary *Ardfert*
Margaret Connor *Listowel*	Johanna Connor *Ballylongford*	Mary Ryan *Listowel*	Biddy Ryan *Listowel*
Mary Conway *Dromkeen E.D.*	Winnie Pierce *Ratoo*	Margaret Scanlon *Listowel*	

Daniel Griffin was voted 'twenty pounds to defray the expenses of the Emigrants to Dublin'.[18] The girls were initially taken with their trunks by cart and train to Dublin's North Wall for boat and train to Plymouth, to board the ship *Thomas Arbuthnot* leaving for Sydney on 28 October 1849.

Each girl was to be provided with a specified list of requirements. All items were to be new and of good quality. Since all the girls were Catholics they were each to be given a Douay Bible. Finally the Guardians were to provide wooden boxes of good material with strong locks into which the girls were to pack their belongings. Each emigrant's name was to be clearly painted on the front of the box. The list of requirements were as follows:

12. September 49

5

The Clerk's Report of Vaccination was read—(this on the first meeting in every month.) Number of successful cases.

The Report of the Visiting Committee was read and Orders were made thereon as follows:

11th September

Lieut Henry this day examined the several Orphan girls in the Work House and selected the following for emigration to Australia:

Mary Conway — Dromkeen Electoral Division
Margaret Cohan — Listowel
Cathre Ryan — Larbert
Eliza Moriarty — Finuge
Honora Sinec — Listowel
Ellen Wilson — do
Mary Wilson — do
Mary Brandon — Newtownsandes
Mary Russell — Listowel
Johana Connor — Ballylongford
Margaret Scanlon — Listowel
Ellen Leary — Ardfert
Winny Purse — Rattoo
Mary Ryan — Listowel
Mary Leary — Finuge
Ellen Carey — Rattoo
Johana Hayes — Kiltomey
Margaret Stack — do
Biddy Ryan — Listowel

Ordered that the requisite outfit &c for those girls be at once provided.

The Reports of the Master and other Officers were read, and Orders made thereon, as follows:

2 The Master made the following Report.

"The Master begs to report that the education of the female children appears to be very much neglected at the Work House school. On yesterday when the Emigration officer examined the girls many of whom had been 2 years at the school, very few could even read very imperfectly, & only one or two make any attempt at writing. The Emigration Officer requested the Master to bring this matter under the serious attention of the Vice Guardians."

The Vice Guardians regret being obliged to bring this Report under the Commissrs notice — In consideration of Miss Nolans excellent Moral character they were heretofore unwilling to remove her from her situation and have therefore endeavoured but in vain endeavoured to stimulate her to a more energetic discharge of her duties —

3 The following Report was also made by the Master

"The Master reports that the Wardsman D. Griffin complained to him last night of the conduct of one of the Wardswomen Mary _____ in seeking from a Pauper man Denis Moran the loan of one shilling to enable _____ woman later a pauper in the House to procure a summons against him for an assault alleged to have been committed by him in the discharge of his duty:"

The Woman referred to Bridget Sullivan was on last Saturday committed by the Magistrates at Petit Sessions to prison for _____

Minutes of the Listowel Board of Guardians, 11 September 1849.

6 Shifts, 6 prs Stockings, 2 prs of shoes, 2 Gowns 2 Short Wrappers, 2 Night
Wrappers, 2 Flannel Petticoats, 2 Cotton Petticoats, 1 Stout Worsted Shawl
& a Cloak, 2 Neck and 3 Pocket Handkerchiefs, 2 Linen Collars, 2 Aprons, 1
Pair of Stays, 1 Pair Sheets, 1 Pair of Mitts, 2 Towels, 2lbs Soap, Combs and
Brushes, Needles, Thread, Tape and articles (such as a few yards of calico)
that the Matron might desire Females to acquire, Books, Bible and Prayer
Book, Bible (Douay).

Each girl also received a paper from the workhouse certifying her good
conduct and unblemished moral character and a medical certificate
showing she was of good health and had been vaccinated against smallpox.

Dingle

While the Dingle Relief Committee was set up in 1845, the actual Dingle
Union did not formally come into being until 22 February 1848. We know
that the Dingle Peninsula was particularly badly affected by the Famine.
Ventry, Ballyferriter and Castlegregory were blackspots on a par with
Skibereen and Kilrush. We know from reports and letters to the *Kerry
Evening Post*, in particular from 1847 onwards, that:

> The state of the people in Dingle is horrifying. Fever, famine and dysentery
> are daily increasing, deaths from hunger are daily occurring. From all parts
> of the country they crowd into the town for relief and not a pound of meal to
> be had in the wretched town for any price.[19]

Prior to 1848, Dingle was part of the Tralee Union. From January 1848
onwards the Poor Law Commissioners were taking seriously the problems
in the Dingle Peninsula and had dispatched Capt. Hotham to report to them
on the situation. Captain Hotham immediately proposed that Dingle Union
be separated from Tralee and that a temporary workhouse be obtained
with a view to erecting a permanent one. He also reported that 'destitution
in the distant divisions' was increasing: 'If we had a workhouse at Dingle,
capable of holding 1,500, it would be filled in a day; but it is never worth-

while for this 1,500 to travel into Tralee for the chance of admission, to return again, if refused.'[20]

On St Patrick's Day 1849, it was recorded in the Minute Books that '9003 destitute persons were relieved out of the workhouse',[21] and by 7 July 1849 that number had increased to 10,481 persons. By September of 1849, the problem of starvation was intensified by the number of famine-related diseases – cholera, smallpox, dysentery and typhus – being experienced with fever hospitals open in Dingle and Castlegregory. On 22 September the Board minuted a resolution 'calling the attention of the Guardians to the overcrowded state of the workhouse, and its auxilia-ries'.[22] Notwithstanding all the problems, a notice went out in the locality asking for tenders for the outfitting of the orphans – 'Resolved that the Clerk be directed to advertise for 40 prs of shoes for the emigrants and for supplying the workhouse and its auxiliaries with mutton for 6 months.'[23] On 5 October we learn that James Sullivan 'be declared contractor for sup-plying 40 pairs of shoes for the Emigrants at a 2s.9d. per pair according to the pattern sent in',[24] and Frances A. Dunlevy got the contract for 'convey-ance of Emigrants to Dublin £20'. James Sullivan's shoes were a bargain, as shoes cost 4s 0d per pair in Kenmare at that time. All these prepara-tions must have been very exciting for the girls who were selected to go. It is very unlikely that any of them would ever have worn shoes, and their clothes before they entered the workhouse were only rags, which neither covered them properly nor provided any protection from the elements. Underclothes were an unknown luxury.

> Stating that the ship which is to convey the Emigrants selected from this Union is to leave Plymouth on 22nd inst and that it will be necessary that these parties should be in Dublin in time for the steamer which is to leave for Plymouth on the 20th inst.[25]

While twenty girls were selected, and Poor Law Commissioners accounts state as such, it was in fact nineteen girls who left Dingle on the first leg of their journey to the North Wall, in Dublin and joined the Listowel girls there for the initial sea journey to Plymouth staying as their companions on the long voyage to Sydney.

Mary Barry	Mary Griffin	Eliza Kenane	Catherine Moriarty
Mary Brien	Julia Harrington	Ellen McGillicuddy	Mary Moriarty
Mary Connor	Mary Kearney	Mary McMahon	Ellen Sheehy
Mary Dowd	Catherine Kennedy	Bridget Moore	Mary Sullivan
Ellen Galvin	Mary Kennedy	Johanna Moore	

Ships Register: Dingle Girls on *Thomas Arbuthnot*

It was reported in the *London Illustrated News*:

> A little colony of female immigrants from the Workhouses of Listowel, Ennis, Dingle and Ennistymon, left the North Wall, Dublin on Sunday for Plymouth, where they are to embark for Australia on a Government Transport. All these poor girls, upwards of one hundred, were comfortably attired and well equipped for the journey.[26]

The Dingle Workhouse was not finished with the orphans, however. It appears that there were shortcuts taken in outfitting the girls and the Matron in Plymouth had to invest in further 'necesseries'. Lieutenant Henry billed the Union for the outstanding amount and asked to remit same by postal order.[27]

Kenmare

Kenmare Poor Law Union covered an area of 423 square miles. The Union was in a remote mountainous area with particular problems of its own. The population of the Union at the time of the Famine, as returned in the Minute Books, was 33,050 with a 'sizeable proportion of these from off the Landsdowne Estate'.[28] The population of the Landsdowne Estate in 1841 within the Kenmare Union had been 16,695 with its absentee Landlord – Henry Petty Fitzmaurice, 3rd Marquess of Landsdowne – living in Bowood, his estate in Wiltshire. Fitzmaurice was a 'strong champion of Catholic and Jewish emancipation, abolition of the slave trade, limited parliamentary reform and national education'.[29] However, his attitude to Ireland was 'the diminution by every means possible of the Irish population, a harsh attitude to famine relief and the belief that the demand for fixity of tenure involved a plot ...'[30]

By early 1847 hunger was not the only affliction suffered in Kenmare. Fever was rampant in the district and particularly in the main workhouse and its auxiliaries. Dr Thomas Taylor, medical officer to the Kenmare Poor Law Union, wrote:

> Our distress in this district is grave indeed ... 100 die daily, painfully of Fever and Dysentery ... which would not have the same force but for previous starvation. At the Poor House I attend daily 200 in the Epidemic. I am unassisted. More than 40 medical officers of the Union Work Houses have already perished of Fever caught in the discharge of their duties. Assuredly my turn cannot be very distant.[31]

Dr Taylor forecast his own demise; he died of fever contracted in the workhouse in February 1848.

The Minutes of the Kenmare Union tell us that on Wednesday 28 August 1849:

> Lt. Colonel Clarke, Poor Law Inspector accompanied by two Guardians, proceeded this day in accordance with instructions, to select a number of orphan girls between the ages of 14 and 18 years for the purpose of emigration to Australia. 41 were deemed eligible and await inspection of the Government Agent.[32]

On that date there 217 'girls' in the workhouse, which would have comprised all able-bodied females over the age of 15.

Life among the Kenmare girls was not always peaceful. Even though the forty-one girls who were deemed eligible were awaiting their 'inspection' by the Emigration Agent, we would expect that none of them were among the 'disorderly women' who created a disturbance in the dining hall on the morning of Wednesday 19 September. James Hickson JP and George Maybury, the workhouse doctor, held an 'extraordinary session in the Sorters Hall at the request of the Vice-Guardians, when Mary Downing, Mary O'Sullivan Stretton, Abby Coughlan and Mary McCarthy were sentenced to one month's imprisonment and hard labour in Tralee Gaol' as a result.[33]

By October 1849, Lieutenant Henry had been to Kenmare and made his selection:

Lieut Henry RN, Emigration Agent having selected 30 Females of whom 25 are to be fitted out for Emigration to Australia and to leave for Plymouth on 29 November, resolved that the forms of consent be affixed in the emigration of the persons therein and to the payment of a portion of the expenses of such emigrants. Cost of the funds of this Union to be now signed and forwarded to the Poor Law Commissioners.[34]

The Kenmare Guardians were most efficient; on the same day they noted that they would advertise by handbill 'inviting tenders for supplying the following articles for the outfit for the females selected for emigration to Australia'. 'Tenders will also be received from Persons willing to contract for making the necessary articles of clothing.' This simple sentence gives us a picture of the designated Kenmare 'bell man' going up and down Henry Street and Shelbourne Street, ringing his bell and giving out his handbills with its requirements for clothing for the orphans for any supplier who might be interested in quoting. And on 12 November the Board took a decision to award the contract to Murty Sullivan for the following:

2/5 yds	Bonnet Ribbon @ 5d. per yard
25	Tooth Brushes @ 5d. each
60 yds	Cap Ribbon @ 2 1/2 per yard
100	Plain Cotton Stockings @ 6d. per pair
200 yds	Cotton for dresses @ 4d. per yard
150 yds	Plaid for dresses @ £1.8.0

Signed: *Ed Godfrey, Chairman*[35]

However, the path of clothing the girls did not run smooth. There should have been able sewing women among the inmates of the workhouse, who would have run up the necessary outfits from the material supplied. Supplying the shoes caused a major problem. On the 17 November we note that:

Timothy Healy, having declined to furnish the shoes for the Emigrants in accordance with his tender for the same accepted by the Guardians on the 13th inst., the tender of Daniel Mahony to supply by the 24th inst., 50 pairs of Girls' shoes at 4s.0d. per pair to be paid for on delivery, was accepted.[36]

We should note here 'to be paid on delivery'. Obviously the credit worthiness of the Union was in doubt among the local shopkeepers. This is reinforced by the story in *Realities of Irish Life*, written by William Steuart Trench (1808–1872), that in the winter of 1849–50, when the number receiving relief in the Kenmare Union were 'somewhere about ten thousand' he was called to a meeting of the Board, of which he was not then a member, to learn that 'a contractor to whom a very large amount of money was due, had positively refused to give another sack of meal unless he received an instalment in cash that day'.[37] While Steuart Trench proposed that all present, including himself, put their hands in their pockets and subscribe and they would take the chance of the Union refunding later, he could not get any volunteers. He consulted with the government officer present and ascertained from him that 'considering the numbers who are depending exclusively on this food, and who are already in the last stage of destitution' that in excess of 'twelve to fifteen hundred persons will be dead before twenty-four hours are over'.[38] As Lord Landsdowne's agent, Steuart Trench was lucky that he had some funds available and was able to pay a portion of the debt and get the meal delivered.

However, the saga of the shoes and clothing continued. Two weeks later there is a note on the minutes: 'A writ was served on the Clerk at the suit of Mrs. Ellen Healy of Kenmare for £420.14.0 with interest, due by the Guardians of the Kenmare Union for materials for clothing the Orphans.'[39] There is no explanation as to the cause for the writ, except Mrs Healy must have been trying to expedite payment of her account.

On the same day, 29 November, we are told 'The following is a list of the female orphans sent from the workhouse on the 29th instant as emigrants to Australia. Their names and ages and distinguishing the electoral division to which the list of emigration is chargeable.'[40]

Mary Connor	Jessie Foley	Ellen McCarthy	Frances Reardon	Mary Shea
Kenmare East	*Kenmare E.*	*Ballybog E.*	*Union at Large*	*Tuosist E.*
Mary Corkery	Margaret Foley	Mary McCarthy	Mary Regan	Mary Sullivan
Union at large	*Kilgarvan E.*	*Kilgarvan E.*	*Tuosist E.*	*Tuosist E.*
Margaret Cronin	Ann Husband	Mary McCarthy	Mary Shea	Catherine Sullivan
Templenoe E.	*Templenoe E.*	*Union at large*	*Kenmare E.*	*Kenmare E.*

Mary Dineen	Ellen Lovett	Margaret Murphy	Julia Shea	Honora Sullivan
Union at Large	Kenmare E.	Tuosist E.	Bonane E.	Tuosist E.
Catherine Downing	Catherine Manning	Mary Murphy	Jane Shea	Margaret Sullivan
Ballybog E.	Templenoe E.	Kenmare E.	Ballybog E.	Kilgarvan E.

Again the girls left Kenmare for Dublin initially, sailing out of Plymouth on the *John Knox* on 6 December and arriving in Sydney on 29 April 1850.

By early 1850 hostility to the entire scheme had built up in Australia. Due to the negative reactions coming from upper- and middle-class opinion and echoed in the national newspapers, the scheme was brought to an end in that year. There were a number of elements involved. There was an inherent anti-Irish, anti-Catholic and anti-female prejudice in the colonies at that time. The orphans were denounced as 'immoral, useless and untrained domestic servants, a drain upon the public purse, a financial liability, who, being blindly devoted to their religion, threatened to bring about a Popish ascendancy in New South Wales and Victoria'.[41] In December 1849 the Orphan Emigration Committee in Australia stated that 200 of the orphans were unemployed and this was mainly due to their inability to perform housework, rather than the earlier charges of immorality.[42]

Added to the general objections as to their suitability was a particular prejudice towards Irish Catholic immigrants, promulgated in the main by Scottish and Northern Irish Presbyterians who had settled in New South Wales from 1840 onwards. Some of these were small landholders who sold their tenant rights and set out to seek a better life in the new colony. They had bought into the new lands available to them, were hard workers and were nervous that they would be out numbered now by Catholics. Their chief spokesman, John Dunmore Lang, then a Member of the legislative council of the colony, wrote to Earl Grey urging the emigration only of 'virtuous and industrious Protestants'.[43]

Margaret Cronin

Margaret Mary Cronin was the third child of Myles Cronin and Honora Clifford ('Cluvane' on her Baptismal Certificate), who were married on 10 February 1820 at Dunkerron in County Kerry.

Margaret was born in 1831, which meant she was 19 years of age when she emigrated, but on arrival her age was recorded as 16. The other children of Myles and Honora were John born 1821, Mary born 1824, Myles born 1837 and Cornelius born 1840. The baptism certificate of Margaret records the following:

Name MARGARET CRONIN

Date of Birth 4 July 1831 [BASED ON OTHER DATE INFORMATION]

Address DUNKERRON

Father MYLES CRONIN	Mother HANORA CLUVANE
Father Occupation NR	Priest REV: R.F.M.
Sponsor 1 DERMOT SULLIVAN	Sponsor 2 MARY SIGERSON

Book	Number	Page	Entry Number Record_Identifier
1	N/R	165	KY-RC-BA-267000

In the Tithe Applotment Books[44] of 1840, Myles Cronin's rent in the townland of Dunkerron, Parish of Templenoe in the Diocese of Ardfert and Aghadoe is £5 10s 0d. By the time of Griffith's Valuation (1848–1851) Myles Cronin's family is no longer a tenant on this land. We would have to presume that both parents had died in the Famine prior to Margaret's selection in Kenmare Workhouse in December 1849.

Margaret arrived on the *John Knox* at Port Jackson on 29 April 1850. Her arrival documentation also states that her parents were 'both dead', she could not read or write and had no relatives in the colony. We have no record of where she was initially apprenticed, but it would appear that she stayed in Sydney and was not moved on to Moreton Bay as a number of the other Kenmare girls were.

Margaret's great-great-grandson Peter Booth tells us that:

Margaret Mary Cronin arrived in Sydney on 29th April 1850 along with over 250 other Irish Orphan girls aboard *John Knox* after a voyage of nearly five months. She would have been assigned as a servant to a family in Sydney.

On 8th January 1856, Margaret Cronin married John William Clark, a carpenter and free settler, who had arrived from Plymouth some three years earlier. They had ten children in various parts of New South Wales including George 1857, Ellen 1858, Ernest 1861, Margaret 1863, Agnes 1865, Kate 1866, Emily 1868, Minnie 1869, John 1872, before Margaret died with her last child in 1873. She is buried at Bathurst, New South Wales.

Descendants include a Deputy Commissioner of Railways, a local mayor and a Prime Minister's secretary. Margaret Cronin has significantly contributed to the fabric of Australia.

Listowel – Second Group of Emigrants

In Listowel, the Board of Guardians were apparently unaware of the situation building up in Australia. On 7 March 1850 an excerpt from the Minutes of their meeting reads:

Resolve that we deem it a matter of incalculable advantage to the Union, to promote by every means, the emigration of the paupers, who are now crowding the Workhouse, not only as a means of providing for the most deserving of those persons, but as to the ultimate relief to the Union and as Lieutenant Henry has selected from among the female orphans of this house, 20 named underneath whom he considers eligible for emigration to Australia, we hereby consent to provide them with necessary outfit as decided upon by the Emigration Commissioners and to defray their expenses to the port of Embarkation ... and the Matron hereby directed to provide the necessary outfits for the following girls.[45]

Mary Courtney	Catherine O'Sullivan	Anne Buckley	Julia Daily
Ellen Leary	Bridget Griffin	Mary Griffin	Margaret Ginniew
Mary Daly	Johanna Scanlon	Deborah Kissane	Catherine Mullowney

Mary Sullivan	Mary Stack	Honora Brien	Mary Creagh
Catherine Connor	Johanna Sullivan	Margaret Connor	Ellen Relihan

Minutes of Listowel Board of Guardians, 7 March 1850

Again the same system of selection and medical checks were carried out. On 8 April 1850 they sailed from Plymouth on the *Tippoo Saib*, an ageing barque of 1,022 tons. The master was Captain W. Morphew. There were 297 orphans in total on board.

Four months later, following brief stops for supplies and water in Tenerife and Capetown, the *Tippoo Saib* was escorted into Sydney Cove on 29 July 1850. Captain Morphew's report to the health authorities in Sydney stated that, of his total passengers, 'one was suffering from lunacy, one had consumption and another hysteria'. Three had died on the voyage from 'exhaustion, nervous irritation and infection of the brain respectively'.[46]

Grave doubts would have to be cast on the selection process, however well-meaning Lieutenant Henry was. Regrettably it would appear that apart from physical appearance, he would have had little choice in

Tippoo Saib *arrivals, 29 July 1850.*

matters of the personal attainments of the unfortunate, virtually uneducated girls. The subsequent shipping records show that on arrival a large
number of the Kerry orphans were unable to read or write. They were
totally untrained in housework, needlework or 'washing', though a few
may have had the rudiments of farm work. At least three of the orphans
were not natives of their Unions. There is no reason to believe that some of
the Guardians would not have interfered in the process, thereby promoting the emigration of unwanted orphans from within their own families
or communities.

The *Tippoo Saib*, with these Listowel girls, was the last of the Earl Grey
Scheme ships bringing Irish orphans to the colonies of New South Wales,
Moreton Bay, Port Philip and South Australia.

❧5❧

BACKGROUND
TO THE GIRLS

T HE ONLY INFORMATION available to us, from workhouse
records, on the background of each individual girl is a name and,
in a few cases, the electoral area from which the girl had been registered when they were selected for the emigration process. However, as
recorded in the example below,[1] the age groups and the capacity of each
inmate for work were included, as were the number admitted each week,
the number already there and the number who died or were discharged.
Also included were the auxiliary workhouses and fever hospital and the
number of 'lunatics and idiots' in the workhouse at each weekly date.

While precise records were kept of all expenditure and the type and
amount of food consumed, there is very little else in the way of identities or
pen pictures of any of the inmates, available to us.

It is only if an inmate caused a row or disturbance that their name
would get a mention. There is a case in Kenmare where Mary Downing,
Mary O'Sullivan Stretton, Abby Coughlan and Mary McCarthy are
named in the minutes as they caused 'a disturbance' and were sentenced
to a month in gaol in Tralee with hard labour (see Chapter 5). We also
have reports in Killarney of an allegation that 'a pauper named Mary
Sullivan' had accused another pauper named Jude Spillane of 'attempts
to induce her to become a protestant'.[2] But other than these few individuals named in the Minutes of Board of Guardian meetings, we have no

STATE of the WORKHOUSE for the Week ending Saturday, the 22.⁰⁰ day of *March* 1851.													
Number of Inmates for which accommodation is provided.	No. that each building. Total No. above date.		Able-bodied.		Aged and Infirm persons, and adult persons, above 15 years of age, but not working.		Boys and Girls above 9 and under 15 years of age.		Children above 5 and under 9 years of age.	Children above 2 and under 5 years of age.	Infants under 2 years of age.		RETURN OF SICK AND LUNATICS.		OBSERVATIONS.
Workhouse, . . .	*1036*	*1638*											Number in Hospital on the above date.	No. of Lunatics and Idiots in Workhouse on the above date.	
Temporary Building, .	*1010*	*787*													
Additional Workhouse, .	*2455*	*2404*													
Fever Hospital	*40*	} *154*													
Fever Sheds, . . .	*66*		Males.	Fem.	Males.	Fem.	Boys.	Girls.				Total.			
Total, . .	*4607*	*4983*													
Remaining on previous Saturday, as per last Return, . .			*665*	*1322*	*61*	*76*	*964*	*929*	*730*	*169*	*40*	*4796*	In Work house Hospital, *558*	In any sick Wards	
Admitted during the Week,			*36*	*61*	*5*	*7*	*25*	*25*	*28*	*11*	*6*	*202*	In Fever Hospital, *166*	In Wards with other Lunatics, *12*	
Total,			*701*	*1383*	*66*	*83*	*984*	*952*	*758*	*170*	*46*	*5148*	Total, *724*	Total, *12*	
Discharged during the Week,			*10*	*44*	*4*	*3*	*15*	*9*	*11*	*2*	*1*	*99*			
Died			*3*	*8*	*1*	*5*	*5*	*12*	*20*	*7*	*5*	*66*	→ N.B. 17 ADULTS AND 49 UNDER 15 YRS (13 FEMALES)		
Total Discharged and Dead,			*13*	*52*	*5*	*8*	*20*	*21*	*31*	*9*	*6*	*165*			
REMAINING ON THE ABOVE DATE,			*688*	*1331*	*61*	*75*	*964*	*931*	*727*	*161*	*40*	*4983*			

Listowel Workhouse weekly returns, 22 March 1851. It records that sixty-six people died this week, seventeen adults and forty-nine under the age of 15 years.

records of inmates, when they entered or how long they stayed in each workhouse.

We have the names and electoral districts of the first lot of girls from Listowel who travelled on the *Thomas Arbuthnot*, and we also have the names and electoral districts of the Kenmare girls who travelled on the *John Knox*. The principal reason for recording the electoral districts, in the case of Kenmare at any rate, was to note which areas were chargeable for the expenses incurred in the emigration process, rather than to keep a precise record of who left and how they left.

However, very precise records were kept in Sydney on the ship's arrival. When the *Thomas Arbuthnot* arrived on 3 February 1850, the *John Knox* on the 29 April 1850 and the *Tippoo Saib* on the 29 July 1850, the girls' names, ages and their home addresses were taken, as well as the workhouses that they originated from. Their parents' Christian names, their religion and their ability (or not) to read and write were also noted. From these records, we are able to match our lists of those who departed to those who arrived.

To the uninitiated, some of these arrival records make no sense. It helps that the researcher speaks and understands the Kerry accent! So when 'Margaret Ginnea' arrived in Sydney on the *Tippoo Saib* and declared she was from 'Stow', we can match her up with 'Margaret Ginniew' who is on the Listowel Workhouse list. Margaret would have told the clerk in Sydney who was taking down her details that she was from 'Shtow', which we who are used to the local idiom understand plainly as 'Listowel'. To add to the confusion, for some reason anyone in North Kerry who was called McKenna was also called 'Ginnea'. Catherine Kennedy gave her address as 'Brandon Bay' and Bridget Moore as 'Cashel', these were respectively from Brandon and Castlegregory. Catherine Manning of 'Kilmoyle' and Ellen McCarthy of 'Kilmajer' we can immediately deduct are respectively from Templenoe, Kenmare and Kenmare itself.

The arrival records state the ages of the girls ranged from 14 to 20 years of age. However, we can see that these ages are very inaccurate when we compare the actual church baptismal certificates of those girls whom we can trace. Birthdays and ages were of very little significance in the nineteenth century. The system of registration of births in Ireland at that time was that the individual was responsible for registering the birth. The authorities, as an 'encouragement' to do this, would impose a hefty monetary fine on the individual who didn't comply with the law. So a birth registration might take some time to be recorded and the exact day, and even year and place might not be correct when it was finally registered. In quite of a lot of cases, particularly in rural, inaccessible country, the birth was never registered. These inaccurate birth dates have persisted through the follow-on records in Australia, resulting in wildly differing birth dates given on marriage, children's baptisms and death certificates. There would not have been any subterfuge or dishonesty intended. When genealogists are conducting research now in Ireland for nineteenth-century ancestors, it is a recognised fact that 'the actual date of birth is almost always well before the one reported, sometimes by as much as fifteen years'.[3]

The vast majority of the girls were probably aged 16 and 17, even though seven girls stated on arrival that they were 14. They were Mary Healy (Killarney), Catherine McCarthy (Killarney), Mary Kearney (Dingle), Margaret Foley (Kilgarvan), Ellen Lovett (Kenmare), Johanna Sullivan (Listowel) and Johanna Donoghue (Killarney), who died at sea while on the *Elgin*, which was bound for South Australia.

It is interesting to note that four of these five girls were recorded as being able to both read and write. This is probably because the younger they were, the more opportunity they would have had of attending the new National Schools which were built from the early 1840s, or they may have attended the hedge schools prior to entry to the workhouse. Of the older girls, close to sixty[4] of the girls could neither read nor write. As most of the girls were also from country areas, Irish would have been their first language, but even if not able to read or write in English they would have understood the language for the most part and have started to speak it.

Of the 117 Kerry girls, 112 were recorded as 'Church of Rome'. Five of the girls gave their religion as Church of England; four of these were from Listowel and one from Kenmare. While researching the background to the girls, each girl was matched with the church records of baptisms in Kerry, through her name, parents' details and parish, if known. This was quite frustrating, as in a number of cases the girls' details did not correspond with the parents' names they had given. While we know that a number of the girls were orphans in the accepted sense, i.e. with both parents dead, in any Union workhouse there would also be a number of girls born outside marriage or certainly baptised before their parents married. These girls would not have necessarily known the names of their fathers. Yet every girl gives the name of both a father and a mother.

Illegitimacy was a taboo subject in nineteenth-century Ireland. Moral, financial and social approbation were all levied against the unmarried mother. She had very few rights and all the responsibilities. The Poor Law Act (1838) placed the sole responsibility for supporting children born outside marriage on the mother, and put the father under no legal obligation to his extra-marital child. Many single mothers had no option but to take refuge in workhouses. Ratepayers who funded the workhouses resented supporting these women and children and an Irish Poor Law Amendment Act was passed in 1862.[5] It empowered Boards of Guardians to recover from a presumed father the cost of maintaining his illegitimate child on the Poor Rates, after the mother had made a sworn statement, supported by corroborative evidence, before petty sessions. The new laws gave no power to the mother to sue the father, and once she left the workhouse the liability of the father ended.[6]

The separation of the moral and respectable women from geographically mobile and subsistent women was essential practice at this time, as it was believed by middle-class men that female immorality was contagious to other women.[7]

In Kerry, different baptismal standards applied in different areas. Baptismal records in the early 1800s were written in longhand in Latin. While generally speaking the name of the admitted father was not included, some priests might write it in or append a side note as *illegitimus* or *pater ignotum* (father unknown). In most cases there would not be an admitted father. In Ballyduff/Causeway between September 1824 and September 1828 the priests who ministered in this area appear to have baptised those born outside marriage by registering boys with the name of Jasper and likewise the girls as Winifred. There is a total of eighteen boys baptised as Jasper and seventeen girls as Winifred during these four years. In February and March 1828 all seven baptisms in the area are called one or other of these names! As these names are never again recorded in this or indeed any other area in Kerry, we will have to presume that the parents (with the exception of Winifred's) didn't use them as everyday Christian names. In these cases of Ballyduff/Causeway there is both a mother and father's surname name on all of the baptismal records, and it is interesting to note that the children born all bore the father's surname.

Among the 117 Kerry girls on the Earl Grey Scheme, there are a number of respectable and well-behaved girls who had been born outside marriage, most of whom would prefer this fact not to be known. They would have wished to start in their new world without any perceived stain and they cannot be blamed for this. Neither could they be blamed for the sins of their parents and there was every likelihood that they would become 'active and useful members of a society which is in a state of healthy progress'.[8]

Dingle

Of the nineteen Dingle girls, we know that twelve declared that both parents were dead, three of the fathers were alive 'in Dingle' and five of the mothers. Of those who were still alive, Mary Barry declared that her father's residence was 'unknown' and her mother lived in Castlegregory. Mary Griffin, whose baptismal certificate states that she is from Ballynabuck, Ballyferritter, says that her mother is 'living near Dingle' which more than likely meant that she was still at home in Ballyferritter. We would have to assume that at least some of those 'alive' were still in the workhouse in

Dingle. The Moriarty sisters – Catherine (17) and Mary (16) – whose parents were both dead, hailed from Dingle town.

The geographic area of Castlegregory and Brandon, whose population is now a quarter of what it was before the Famine, both coastal areas, suffered more than most during the Famine. The journey to obtain food and/or shelter, initially to Tralee and later to Dingle over unmade roads through mountain passes, was one of unimaginable hardship. Mary Barry, Julia Harrington, Bridget Moore and Catherine Kennedy, with their families, had to trudge to the workhouse, in a cold, hungry, unclothed and shoeless state, the long miles without any guarantee of getting help at the end.

It has not been possible to trace a number of the Dingle girls, principally those who were baptised in the town, as the extant records are illegible from March 1828 to April 1833, a period when most of the girls concerned were baptised. At a future date, with newer technology, it may be possible to retrieve these important records.

Mary Griffin

Mary Griffin was born 16 March 1831 in the parish of Ballynabuck in Ballyferriter, Dingle to John Griffin and Mary Sullivan. There were at least five more children recorded in the Baptismal registers:

1. John Griffin – Baptised 3 march 1829
2. Mary Griffin – Baptised 16 march 1831
3. Maurice Griffin – Baptised 31 March 1834
4. ? Griffin – Baptised 11 September 1836
5. Johanna Griffin – Baptised 14 September 1839
6. Catherine Griffin – Baptised 13 April 1843

She was one of twenty girls selected from Dingle Workhouse to travel to Australia on the Earl Grey Scheme. On arrival, her records tell us that 'her mother was living near Dingle', and that she 'cannot read or write'. To be fair to Mary, Irish would have been her first and perhaps only language and it may be that she could not read or write English. Her age is correctly given as 19.

We would presume that her father was dead by autumn 1849, when she was selected. There is no evidence now available that her siblings were alive then, perhaps also in the workhouse, or that they had died from hunger or from one of the many fevers and diseases that swept through the population.

Mary was one of the lucky girls; she was taken by Surgeon Charles Strutt with 108 others on a journey into the interior of New South Wales where Strutt carefully vetted all the applicants for servants. If he felt that they would not get a good home and be treated properly, he had no compunction if refusing employers or indeed removing the girls to better employers.

Mary's great-great-grandson Nathan Brown tells us:

Mary Griffin was employed by landowner William Grogan of Sawyer's Flats, near Yass (West of the Burrowa river; east of Sawyer's Creek; south of Hassall's Creek; north of the colony's boundary line) for one year on £8. The land was roughly 9,700 acres and was estimated to have the capability of grazing 400.

Less than one year later, Mary married William Dixon [Dickson, Dixson] (also of Sawyer's Flats) on the 2nd March, 1851 at St. Augustine's Roman Catholic Church, Yass.

Mary Griffin and William Dixon had two children, Ellen Dixon who was born about 1852 in Yass and died on 4th May in Rye Park, New South Wales. She married David Percival in 1872 at Binalong, New South Wales. David was unusually for the times, a native Australian, born in Sydney in 1845, the son of William Ambrose Percival and Anne Semple. David died at his home in Campbell St., on 24 December 1933 having been stricken down two weeks earlier by a paralytic stroke. He was buried on Christmas Day. Ellen Dixon and David Percival had fourteen children.

While all the 'orphans' experienced loneliness, those who settled in the areas around Yass were probably the most fortunate. A number of Mary's shipmates from the *Thomas Arbuthnot* were settled there, including a number of the Dingle girls. The main route from Sydney to Melbourne passed through the town, so it was an important place of commerce and was the centre of widespread Catholic and Anglican parishes. Yass was the place where the families from the outlying areas got together for the big events in life – baptisms, marriages and funerals in the local churches. The settlers in the outlying bush districts also came to Yass a couple of times a year for their supplies.

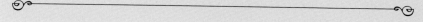

Listowel

The Wilson sisters, who were on the Listowel list, also recorded their parents as both dead. The Wilson girls were registered as Church of England and as there are no baptismal certificates for them in the Kerry area, we would have to assume that they were introduced to Listowel Workhouse by one of the Church of England guardians. Margaret Raymond and Julia Daly from Listowel also declared their religion as Church of England.

We know that Margaret Raymond was not initially selected by Lieutenant Henry, but she seems to have been treated as a special case. On arrival in Sydney, she claims to be a cousin of James Raymond, Postmaster General of Australia. Indeed the records bear out this claim as the truth. Margaret states that her parents were William and Hanora (both dead). There is no Church of England or Catholic baptismal record extant for Margaret but a William Raymond and Honora Barrie are registered as the parents of a William Raymond in the Catholic Parish Church Listowel on 12 February 1828, and it is possible that this is Margaret's brother. This William Raymond was later married to Anne Reeves and had further children baptised as Anglicans in Listowel. William Raymond's first cousin, James Raymond, had married and taken up residence in County Limerick but suffered some land troubles. Raymond seems to have had access to some of the most prominent names in the New South Wales colony in the nineteenth century and July 1824 Henry Gouldburn wrote on his behalf to Earl Bathurst, requesting a free passage for Raymond and his family to New South Wales because of their misfortunes in Ireland. This request bore fruit and in 1826 Raymond emigrated to New South Wales. Governor (Sir) Ralph Darling was asked to provide Raymond with a suitable colonial appointment and, until it became available, to allow him the means of subsistence.[9] In 1829 he was appointed Postmaster General.

At the time of Margaret's arrival in February 1850, James Raymond lived in some splendour at Varroville, near Campbelltown, which he had bought from Charles Sturt and there entertained extensively. He died at Darlinghurst on 29 May 1851 aged 65, and was buried at St Peter's, Cook's River. He and his wife Aphra had seven daughters and four sons, of whom James and Robert Peel held positions in the Post Office and William was a landholder at Bathurst. However, there are no records that any of these Raymond cousins made any effort to look out for Margaret or to get her any employment. A month after arriving, having been apprenticed to John Beit in Sydney, he asked to be relieved of her 'because she is insane'.[10] She was then sent on to Moreton Bay and can't have been too 'insane' as she was immediately indentured to the Import Agent and later Chief Constable, G. Watson. Margaret married Patrick Ambrose, an Irish convict, in the Church of England at Ipswich in 1852, and after his death, in 1861, she married again to David Kynoch. Margaret lived until 1912 and died at the ripe old age of 89.

Another Listowel girl who claimed her father was in Sydney was Bridget (Biddy) Ryan. Biddy was the last name on the list selected by Lieutenant Henry, so we would have to presume that she met the rule of being at least one year in Listowel Workhouse, but on arrival in Sydney she gave her 'native place' as Bruff, County Limerick. Her father was called Lancelot (Lanty) Ryan. He had been a soldier but he had been convicted of being a bigamist and, aged 35, he was tried in July 1837 at Limerick Assizes and sentenced to seven years' transportation. In a report of the court case in the *Limerick Chronicle* of 12 July 1837, Fr Halpin PP Bruff, stated that he married 'the prisoner' to Mary Hynes (Biddy's mother) in Bruff and F. Lyddy PP, stated that he had married 'the prisoner' to Jane Huddy in Abbeyfeale at a later date. 'Jane Huddy deposed that she had married the prisoner and that six weeks later his former wife walked in with her family'.[11] The convict ship *Neptune* which departed Dublin on 27 August 1837 for the 128-day voyage to Sydney listed Lancelot as having two children, one male and one female, he was a soldier labourer, and was blind in his left eye.[12] It is possible that Biddy may not have known of her father's conviction. He should have served his sentence and got his ticket of leave by 1844 but we have no record of their ever meeting.

Another interesting 'selection' from Listowel was Julia Daly. On arrival at Sydney on *Tippoo Saib* on 29 July 1850, Julia gives her native place as

Tralee and her religion as Church of England. She could read and write and said she was a dressmaker. However, her baptismal certificate giving her father as Henry O'Daly and her mother as Elizabeth Howard is registered at the Catholic parish church in Tralee. Julia Daly was named in a court case reported in the *Sydney Morning Herald*[13] under the Masters and Servants Act. She was accused of absconding from her employer, a Sydney solicitor named Mr McCulloch of Elizabeth Street, and bringing with her another of the orphans, Mary Connor, also of Listowel. The evidence was not in dispute and it appeared that Captain Morphew, who was the Captain of the *Tippoo Saib*, on which they had arrived, settled Julia in 'a furnished house in Newtown' with Mary Connor as their maid and he had represented Julia as his wife. By the time the case came to court, Captain Morphew had sailed on the return journey to England. While no doubt there were repercussions for his career as a responsible ship's captain, it was the Irish orphans who bore the brunt of the disapproval of the courts and newspaper.

The author's kinswomen Catherine Mullowney [sic] is another mystery woman. She was the daughter of William Mallowney [sic] and Honora Doherty and was baptised in Killarney on 6 April 1830. Her parents had married in the parish church in Killarney on 1 October 1826 and she had brothers and sisters. How or why did she end up in Listowel Workhouse, recording on arrival that her father was 'living in Listowel' and her native place as Millstreet, Cork? She also stated that she had two cousins, James and Denis Mullowney, living in Sydney.

Kenmare

The Kenmare girls had the highest number of what we would regard as real orphans. Only Catherine Sullivan's parents were both alive. Both parents of twenty-two of the Kenmare girls were dead, while Jessie Foley and Margaret Murphy's mothers were 'living at Kenmare'. Kenmare also had the highest number of those who could not read or write. Only Jessie Foley, Frances Reardon and Ellen Lovett were literate.

We can take it that the majority of these Kerry girls came from homes where parents had either died or deserted, or the parents had not married.

There is no doubt from what we know of conditions in their localities that starvation and fever had decimated their communities; they either entered the workhouse with their families, some of whom would still have survived there, or they were abandoned by one or other parent in the hope that they would get food and shelter that the parent was unable to supply. Their lives for the previous four years would have been a constant search for food and shelter. They would have wandered through their local townlands, eventually making it to their nearest workhouse, shoeless and usually dressed in rags. We have the testimony of the Quakers and William Forster in particular, who after his tour of Ireland in 1847 issued an appeal to the women of England to make, prepare and collect clothes to send to the Central Relief Committee for distribution among the destitute in Ireland. 'Many more of those visited [by the Quakers] were widows with young children. In most cases the families had no food, no beds, no fire, little furniture and hunger was so far advanced that many nursing mothers had ceased to lactate. Shortage of clothing was also seen as a problem, as the heads of the families were unable to seek work when they did not have adequate clothing'.[14]

There is no doubt that the inmates of the workhouses and in particular these young girls were there only because it was a last resort for food and shelter and that they were deserving of the opportunity to get out and start a new life on the other side of the world. Whether they were equipped to take on the tasks that awaited them there is another question, though their background, with its deprivations and challenges, would have prepared them for the pioneering spirit which would require 'plenty of honest perspiration and unglamorous toil, a quality of silent heroism and the capacity to endure heartbreak'[15] that Sid Ingram said of later Irish emigrants to Australia.

Margaret O'Sullivan (Cooper)

Margaret O'Sullivan left Kenmare Workhouse on 6 December 1849 initially travelling to Plymouth and then to Sydney. She travelled on the *John Knox*, arriving on 29 April 1850.

We know from the note on the Kenmare Board of Guardians Minutes that Margaret was from Kenmare East Division. When she arrived in Sydney, her arrival papers tell us that she was aged 20, her parent were 'Connor & Mary, both dead'. She could not read or write and had 'no relatives in the colony'.

Kilgarvan is a village in south-east County Kerry near the Cork boundary. It is mountainous country with little fertile land. Sullivan is by far the most common name in that part of Kerry. In Griffith's Valuation of 1852, there were eighty-seven families of Sullivan or O'Sullivan in Kilgarvan parish. Many of these Sullivans are descendants of the O'Sullivan Beare Clan. Their castle at Dunboy was besieged by English forces in 1602, when their leader Donal Cam O'Sullivan Beare, Prince of Beare – a Gaelic princely title – was defeated and the entire garrison killed or executed. The story of the epic journey of Donal and 1,000 of his followers, who fled north to Breffne, on foot, in the depths of winter, has been kept alive in plays and books for the past 400 years. When they reached their destination only thirty-five had survived.

Margaret's baptismal certificate of 15 July 1829 gives her home address as Keelbunau [sic], Kilgarvan and her parent are named as Cornelius and Mary Sullivan. We have ascertained that her family were known as the Sullivan (Coopers) to differentiate the many different Sullivan families in the area. In Griffin's Valuation 1852, we presume that Cornelius had died as it was Mary Sullivan who was leasing 76 acres, 1 rood and 9 perches, shared with one other, from the immediate lessor Richard H. Orpen. While Margaret's arrival documentation says that her mother was dead, this may have been a necessary story to immigration as this was, after all, the Earl Grey 'Orphan Scheme'.

In 1849 in Kilgarvan, most of the families living there were subsistence farmers, eking a living out of their small plots. We don't know what happened to Margaret's parents – did they reach the workhouse and die there from disease or hunger or did they die at home and as a result Margaret had no option but to enter the workhouse? There was great distress in this area during the famine.

The Kenmare girls starting out for Cork must surely have had mixed emotions. They were leaving all they were familiar with, in the depths of winter, travelling by horse-drawn cart through some of the worst affected famine-stricken districts of West Cork to be put on a boat at Penrose Quay in the city, an experience that must have been as frightening as it was exciting.

After the usual short stay in Plymouth they departed on the *John Knox* for Sydney. Shortly after arrival in Sydney Cove, Margaret, with others from the same ship, was put on a steamer and sent north to Moreton Bay. This district in those early days of free settlement was a rough, tough place and many of the Kerry 'orphans' who arrived there and were placed, had trouble with their employers. There are many Court cases reported in the local newspapers where girls were accused of absconding or being 'insolent' towards their mistresses. The girls were well able to defend themselves and in most cases succeeded in getting their indentures cancelled, which gave them the opportunity of moving on to other, and hopefully better employers. They also probably quickly realised that they were being paid below the going rate. Margaret would have been paid £10 with her board, but we know that in 1850 single females were getting £15 to £20, depending on their previous experience.

In any case, the majority of the girls were married within a year or two of arrival. Their husbands were generally older men and almost all were ex-convicts – Tickets of Leave men. They were shepherds, bushrangers, drovers and stockmen and a few were squatters. The girls moved with their husbands from station to station depending on the work and the work depended on the weather – drought, floods, fire all affected economic life. Trevor McClaughlin, in his seminal work *Barefoot & Pregnant?*, outlines very clearly the advantages as well as the disadvantages of being sent to the Moreton Bay district. He explains that the Irish 'orphans' in Brisbane in 1851 were in the 'midst of a supportive community'.[16] The entire white female population at that time 'numbered only 1,053; the Irish orphans were a significant proportion, constituting approximately 10 per cent of the total. The local Catholic priest, Fr Hanly, contributed to their ethnic cohesion, he apparently attended court when they appeared'.[17]

Noni Rush, Margaret's great-great-granddaughter tells us about Margaret's life in Australia:

We have no record of where Margaret was apprenticed but we know that she married Edward Sullivan ex-convict within six months. They were married in the Catholic Church in Ipswich, in January 1851, both putting their X mark on the register. The witness at the marriage was Mary Penn. Mary had only just married John Penn in December 1850. Her maiden name was Mary Lovett. A Mary Lovett had arrived on the *John Knox* with Margaret – she was an orphan as well, native place was listed as Meath. I have also positively identified John Penn as being a convict whose ticket of leave in 1846 required him to stay in the Moreton Bay district. He was quite a bit older than Mary and from Gloucestershire.

At the time of writing, I am still uncertain about Edward Sullivan, who was definitely Irish and a convict. There are a number of 'Edward Sullivans' all convicts transported from Ireland and it is difficult to say with certainty, almost two hundred years later, which one Margaret married. It must have seemed to her though that she was getting the ideal husband – her namesake – a Sullivan from Ireland. However, it turned out that he was not the best material for a husband and the marriage did not last long.

Edward and Margaret seem to have parted company sometime after their children Edward and Ellen were born in the 1850s and from 1860 she lived with James Cosgrove, also an ex-convict. He seems to have been a decent man and treated her well.

James however, had a chequered background also. His parents were John Cosgrove and Eileen Mulvaney, from Carrickadhurish, Longford, Co. Westmeath. He had been convicted at Longford Assizes on July 1839 of being complicit in the murder of his Grandfather James Mulvaney. His Uncle James Mulvaney Jnr, was convicted of the murder and sentenced to hang and he was executed on 3 August 1839. James being only 14 years at the time was sentenced to transportation for life.

Reading reports of the case which was heard in Longford, there was no direct evidence that James was culpable, other than he knew what happened and may have been present at the time of the murders.[18]

James Cosgrave: Alias: Cosgrove   Religion: Catholic
Age on arrival: 15

Marital status: Single
Calling/trade: Errand boy
Born: 1825   Native place: Longford Co
Tried: 1839 Longford   Sentence: Life
Ship: Nautilus (2) [1840]   Crime: Murder wilful

He left Kingstown 17 September 1839 on the ship *Nautilus* with 200 other convicts. One of the convicts died on the journey. They arrived in Port Jackson February 1840, and almost immediately departed for Norfolk Island on 22 February 1840, with 199 convicts on board. Norfolk Island, a notorious penal settlement was a small island in the Pacific between Australia, New Zealand and New Caledonia, which had been colonised by the British in 1778.

Margaret and James Cosgrove settled initially at Blue Nobby Station. They had a number of children but never married, presumably as Margaret was already married to Edward Sullivan. This must have been a slur on respectability in Australia as it was in Ireland and they went to immense efforts to cover it up. They may also have been covering up James' colourful background. In this effort, she often used her former patronymic name of Margaret Cooper rather than Margaret Sullivan, on her children's certificates, leading her descendants, even her immediate family, to believe that her name was Margaret Cooper from Kerry. However, when she died in 1914, her death certificate was in the name of Margaret Sullivan, which of course was her legal married name.

Noni Rush continues the story:

Margaret's life with James was the typical station life – I can only surmise as to when they went to Toenda, but I think James Jnr., bought it and took his parents there to live with his family – it's also interesting to note how the parish map has recorded James Cosgrove as James Cosgrove Jnr, inferring they were well aware they had to distinguish between father and son. The shepherd's life in the early days before fencing could be isolated and often dangerous – stations were like small towns with the main homestead and cluster of slab huts, a central store for buying extra goods besides your weekly rations (typical rations could be 10lbs. of salted mutton or beef, 10lbs. of flour, 2lbs. of sugar and ¼ lb. tea) –

later schools started to be seen as essential – sheep could be divided into flocks of about 1500 – each shepherd took his flock out about an hour after sunrise and remain with it all day, keeping the flock together, finding good pastures and protecting it from dingoes and human marauders – at night they would combine a couple of flocks and make fences out of brush hurdles and a watchman would guard them – the wage would have been roughly about 20 pounds per year

As James was always documented at Blue Nobby as being a shepherd, this was what his life would have been like in the early days – it is possible they could have lived away from the central homestead, but all in all not a bad life to what they would have had in Ireland! Later when they introduced fencing his working life would have changed, but I'd say it would have always have been a station labouring life – the men depended on the women to raise the children and do all those household chores, tending a garden etc. – if anything happened to the mother, a man had to find a woman very quickly to replace her for the children's sake because these stations were vast.

I don't know if James and Margaret ever acquired their own land or if it was just James Jnr who acquired Toenda – on each of James Snr's death certificates he is described as both a labourer and a grazier.

From such humble beginnings for both of them they and their children became successful, well-known and respected members of their community. After a very bad start, James Cosgrove does not appear ever to have been in trouble once he came to Australia – and after a maybe rocky start in the colony for Margaret, once she teamed up with James she seemed to be able to settle to raising a family in a stable environment.

I loved to be able to see that she helped my great-grandmother, Ellen, have her babies – Ellen would have had plenty of people around her at both Tulloona and Yallaroi stations (they were huge stations) but it was her mother who came over from a nearby station (possibly still at Blue Nobby in the 1880s?) to be with her – this would also have to mean Margaret was quite adept at assisting with births.

Any of Margaret's children that I have been able to trace did well in life: Her firstborn, Edward (Uncle Ted), owned land at Boomi and brought up a large family with his wife Martha – when Edward married

Margaret's daughter Ellen and her husband.

it was at Ellen's father-in-law's house so everyone must have been very close – the Schmidt's had worked for years on Yallaroi Station.

My great-grandmother Ellen, Margaret's eldest daughter, became a housemaid at Tulloona Station and married the carpenter, John Henry Schmidt – they must have been valued employees to have been married in the homestead. Theirs was a very successful partnership with John Henry working at Tulloona and Yallaroi until they purchased their own land in Boolooroo Shire in 1898. Tulloona is a homestead on the banks of the Croppa Creek in north-east New South Wales. Its closest capital city is actually Brisbane in Queensland about 330km to the east-north-east with Sydney about 570km away to the south of Tulloona. Likewise

Yallaraoi was a 202,000-acre station in 1840 and is located in north-east New South Wales.

Even though Ellen was illiterate all her life, I can see from a couple of letters she dictated, that she had quite a sharp mind for farm business – she carried on with the property for a number of years after John Henry's death, helped by her sons.

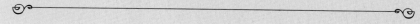

≈6≈

VOYAGE AND ARRIVAL

THE EARL GREY Scheme was a well-run scheme from the point of view of the care and attention put into the outfitting, conveying and shipping of the emigrants to Australia. Each ship carried a Surgeon, School Mistress and where possible a chaplain or religious instructor.

Stringent rules and regulations were drawn up by the Colonial Land and Emigration Commissioners, dealing with the most minute details of life on board 'emigrant passenger ships proceeding from the United Kingdom to any of Her Majesty's Possessions abroad.'[1] The first rule ordered that every passenger was to rise at 7 a.m., unless otherwise permitted by the surgeon. 'Fires to be lighted by the passengers' cook at 7am'. The rules continued, taking into account all and every event that could possibly occur throughout the day until 'the passengers were to be in their beds at 10pm'. A great number of rules were taken up with the necessity of keeping the ship clean, who was responsible for the different duties and exactly the time at which they should be carried out. Interesting rules that do not apply on board ships today state the 'no spirits or gunpowder be taken on board by any passenger' and 'no hay or loose straw to be allowed below'. Religion was taken very seriously and while 'all gambling, fighting, riotous or quarrelsome behaviour, swearing and language, to be at once put a stop to' so also must all passengers 'be mustered on Sundays at 10am, when they will be expected in clean and decent apparel. The day to be observed as religiously as circumstances will permit'.[2]

School hours were to be fixed by the religious instructor or, if no religious instructor, by the surgeon. Teachers were to be exempt from cleaning duties and there was a list of gratuities which would be paid at the end of the journey if the teachers had performed their duties to the satisfaction of the surgeon and the colonial authorities. The teacher's gratuity 'was not to exceed £5'.[3]

The Colonial Land and Emigration authorities were scrupulous also in the arrangements they put in place in Plymouth, for the health, safety and welfare of the girls. Prior to sailing their health was assessed, taking into account the long voyage ahead. They were inspected for cleanliness and their 'boxes' were examined to check that the contents were in place as per the notice issued earlier to the workhouses. The matrons in charge had no compunction in replacing what they considered as inferior clothing and sending the bill back to Ireland. The surgeon superintendents were the people wholly responsible for the moral and physical welfare of the girls and a bonus of 12s 6d was offered for each 'orphan' landed alive. The diet drawn up for the four-month voyage was an improved version of that already being fed to ordinary emigrants. The daily ration of half a pound of beef, pork or preserved meat as well as bread, sugar, tea and coffee was to cause physical upsets to the Irish girls, who had not been used to this quantity and quality of food in their Irish workhouses.

Rules were also drawn up for the conduct of the emigrants' chaplain on arrival at Sydney. The chaplain was to visit 'as speedily as possible' and to 'enter into communication with such of the passengers as may be members of the Church of England'. We would presume with the rivalry prevalent between different churches that the other denominations exercised similar visits to the ships as soon as they arrived in port.

Winifred Pierse

Winifred Pierse with an address in Causeway was baptised in Ballyduff, County Kerry on 17 December 1826. Her parents on the baptismal register are recorded as David Pierse and Bridget Cantlon. The priest in the

Causeway/Ballyduff area at this time, Fr Eoghan McCarthy, disapproving of births outside marriage, christened all the girls born thus with the name of 'Winifred' and all the boys as 'Jasper'.

The parish of Causeway comprises the older parishes of Killury and Ratoo but it is now divided administratively between Causeway and Ballyduff, each with its own church and presbytery. This confusing background must have led Winnie Pierse as she was then known, on arrival in Sydney to give her parents' names as 'David and Ellen', her age as 19, her address as Rattoo, Ballyduff, Kerry. This record also tells us that she could not read or write. Winnie was in fact 24 years of age, over the actual limit of qualifying for an Earl Grey passage. She may have genuinely not known her age or she may have reduced it to qualify or she may have been supported by one of the Board of Guardians to enable her to get selected

Winnie was one of the girls who travelled on with Dr Strutt on the long journey to Yass. She was employed by J. Riordan of Gundagai at £8 a year.

She married William Hines Carrigg on 21 January 1851 at the Roman Catholic church in Yass, New South Wales. William was born about 1800 in Gort, County Galway, Ireland. They settled in Gundagai, where they had nine children: Bridget (1852), Ellen (1853), Ann (1856), William (1858), Ellen (1859), Mary A. (1862), Winifred (1864), Georgina (1866) and Frances (1869). William died in 1875 and Winifred in 1899 in Gundagai. Winifred and her family are included in 'The Eden/Monaro Pioneers database'.

An interesting fact here is that there is an obituary of a John Pierse recorded in the *Adelong and Tumut Express* and *Tumbarumba Post* of Friday 1 July 1921:

After a good and useful life of 87 years, Mr. John Pierse, the squire of 'Shadybrook', Darbalara, died quietly at his home. Deceased's only sister Mrs. W. Carrigg, Gundagai, died many years ago ... John Pierse was like so many of the early Irishmen that came to Australia – a good citizen, straight, religious and clean living – an example to the younger generation of what constitutes one of Nature's gentlemen.

Did Winifred send for her brother? Apparently he was initially a policeman in the late 1850s 'in the stirring days of the gold escort' and then he

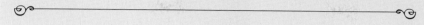

selected land at Darbalara. That he came to live in the same area as Winifred suggests that she had some influence in his decision to settle there

By May 1848 the scheme was in place and W. Stanley, secretary to the Poor Law Commissioners, was able to tell Dublin Castle that Earl Grey's wishes had been fulfilled; 185 young females had been selected from workhouses in northern counties and their departure was imminent. In this letter of 24 May 1848 he also outlined an important fact; that his board hoped that his Excellency the Lord Lieutenant would approve of a decision they had taken. They wished to include in the overall scheme, 'candidates who have one parent living, where the surviving parent, as well as the candidate herself, are both willing that the latter should take advantage of the preferred free passage, not just girls, both of whose parents were dead',[4] which was the original criteria of the Emigration Commissioners. He added that if this proposal was not accepted 'there is reason to fear that the full number for which free passage has been offered, will not be supplied'.[5] This statement was made after the majority of the Unions had replied to the Poor Law Commissioners with lists of girls, showing us that there were more girls in workhouses with one parent living than those with both parents dead at this time.

The first ship to leave for Australia on the scheme was appropriately enough called the *Earl Grey*, which left Plymouth on 3 June 1848 and docked in Sydney four months later on 6 October 1848.

There was immediate controversy on arrival. The girls on this ship were mostly from the northern counties of Ulster and it would appear that the surgeon superintendent, Dr Douglass, had an unhappy experience with them. How much of his later evidence was exaggerated is uncertain but he claimed that many on the boat were not orphans, that some were married, that they came from the 'lowest grade of society and that many of them had been common prostitutes'. In a letter to Governor Fitzroy written the day after arrival he complained that the girls were notoriously bad characters. In order to get these supposedly bad characters out of the way and out of the public eye, thirty-seven of the more troublesome girls were put on a steamer for Moreton Bay, now known as Brisbane.

Moreton Bay had been conceived initially as a penal colony. Up to 1831 only hardened criminals had been sent to this convict community. It had a reputation as one of the harshest penal settlements resulting in a large number of deaths from malaria, prison breakouts, attacks from the native Aborigines and it was generally a tough and inhospitable territory. As well as convicts, two ships which berthed in Moreton Bay in 1849 and 1850 brought 517 Ticket of Leave men from Norfolk Island. Thomas Keneally points out the result of this shipment was 'men let loose on the small towns of Brisbane and Ipswich, where they celebrated being free and on dry land by happily patronising hostelries and generally running amok.'[6] However, in 1838, with the discovery of a fertile hinterland, vast areas of land were opened up to free settlers and in the same year that the first Irish orphans arrived in Sydney, the first emigrant ship with free settlers, the *Artemesia*, arrived to Moreton Bay.

During the two years that the Earl Grey 'Orphan' Scheme was in place, Moreton Bay continued to be a location where the girls who were considered troublesome or difficult to place were sent. The main reason for this was that the colonial authorities wanted to minimise the negative publicity that might cause a further backlash against this scheme supported by the Imperial Government but paid for by the colony.

Eight more Famine 'Orphan' ships were to leave with girls from Irish workhouses, before any of the Kerry girls were to start on their voyage. One year on from the first departure, thirty-five girls left Killarney to travel initially to Penrose Quay in Cork, from there to Liverpool and on to Plymouth, where they departed, 31 May 1849 on the *Elgin* for South Australia. There were 196 Irish orphans among the passengers when it arrived at McLaren Wharf, Port Adelaide on 12 September 1849.

On the day of arrival, the *South Australian Register* recorded: 'The female orphans on board the *Elgin* expressed themselves highly satisfied with their treatment and the Captain says he has not a fault to find with the young women'.[7]

He also had to report that one of his passengers had died at sea. This was Johanna Donahue (*sic*) one of the Killarney girls. Unfortunately it would appear that no proper details were taken on arrival, or if they were they have not survived. For all of the later Kerry arrivals in New South Wales, details of where each of the girls had come from, their parents' names, their reading/writing ability or their religion were meticulously recorded.

There seems to have been a rudimentary age given to each of these girls on arrival in Adelaide. As a result, we cannot say with absolute certainty that Johanna was one of the Killarney girls but we have a baptism recorded in Killarney for a Johanna Donoghue on 8 February 1835 and her parents were Thomas & Johanna Donoghue, which are the names recorded on the ship's manifest. To compound the identification problem, the list of girls selected and compiled by the Killarney Board of Guardians for the Poor Law Commissioners and Colonial Land and Emigration Board has also gone missing. While it is referred to on at least two occasions in the minutes of the Killarney Board of Guardians, it has not survived.

Three days after arrival the Office of the Children Apprenticeship Board, who were the body vested with receiving, placing and the ongoing steward-ship of the orphans, advertised:

> The *Elgin*, with female orphans arrived. Applicants desirous of availing themselves of their Services, are requested to attend in person or by proxy at the Office of the Secretary, Native School on and after Friday next, the 14th instant. It is recommended that the orphans be removed immediately after the arrangements have been made. Signed M. Moorhouse, Secretary to the Board.[8]

Conditions in Adelaide were fairly basic at this time. The town had only been in existence a bare thirteen years. However, both the capital and the state of South Australia had been carefully planned. Land was sold to set-tlers rather than given away free. Dependable and experienced labourers and farmers were the preferred immigrant, rather than convicts and paupers. It was expected that these labourers would work and save and eventually buy land for themselves and their families. There had been good times and bad times for these settlers, with depressions and droughts but after a series of good harvests, at the time of the *Elgin*'s arrival, Adelaide was a busy centre.

From newspaper reports, it appears that the *Elgin* stayed at its moorings in McLaren Wharf. The road into Adelaide was barely a track and almost impassable at this time, but a certain number of girls must have come into the 'Native School', which was the depot from which they could be hired. There seems to have been very little care taken of any of the Irish orphans who arrived in Adelaide and as a result these girls were the ones who had the most trouble in getting employment, in keeping their jobs and generally in behaving in what was known as a 'seemly manner'.

The second lot of Kerry girls, who departed from Dingle and Listowel the following month, and set sail from Plymouth on 28 October 1849, were by far the most fortunate. Their good fortune was entirely down to one man: the surgeon superintendent appointed, Charles Edward Strutt. Dr Strutt has left us a diary of the voyage and of his later journey with 108 of the girls into the Australian interior.

Seventeen girls from Listowel and twenty from Dingle initially went by 'cart' to Dublin. The girls, equipped with their wooden boxes complete with 'strong locks', were conveyed to the North Wall to embark on a steamer for Plymouth. On the steamer they met with girls from workhouses in Dublin, Clare and Galway. The *Thomas Arbuthnot* was a fast sailing ship and one of the largest of the emigrant ships taking settlers and migrants to Australian ports in the 1840s and 1850s. The master of the ship was G.H. Heaton.

The voyage on the *Thomas Arbuthnot* was not Strutt's first encounter with emigrant ships. He had previously served on the *St Vincent*, departing London in October 1848 with Bounty Emigrants for Sydney. These were mostly families and reading his diary of that journey, he had almost constant trouble with a number of the single women as well as some of the single men. Not only was he the ship's doctor but he was also responsible for the moral and physical wellbeing of all the Government emigrants. As well as refusing to scrub out their quarters, some of the single men were far too keen on visiting the single women's dormitory after hours. He had solutions for both misdemeanours. He battened down the hatches of the women's quarters at 8 p.m. each night and any transgression was punished by denying 'puddings' to the passenger concerned as well as a stiff talk. His other responsibility meant that he had to 'settle divers quarrels amongst the emigrants, which is a daily occurrence. I hear both parties and administer a private admonition to the offender.'[9] On Friday 17 November 1848, he reported 'A grand row took place with an Irish family, which after passing through the usual stages of personal abuse, was nearly ended by personal fighting.'[10]

As a surgeon superintendent, Strutt had a wide-ranging job specification. He took his responsibilities very seriously and saw himself as 'preserving order, securing cleanliness and ventilation'. He believed firmly that keep-

Logbook of passengers on the Thomas Arbuthnot, *1850.*

ing the highest standard of hygiene on board would stop a great many of the diseases that were then prevalent, particularly in overcrowded, poorly ventilated places. Strutt was a fair though firm supervisor and he was also a very caring and considerate person.

Strutt showed his compassionate nature even before the *Thomas Arbuthnot* sailed. On arriving at the depot at the Baltic Wharf, he examined the girls but was not happy with the appearance of a number of them. He ordered 'a warm bath for a great number of them, and about 130 to have their hair cut'.[11] Having ascertained that the vast majority of the girls were Roman Catholic, on the day before sailing he called on 'the Romish priest and got a dispensation for the Catholics on board to keep all days alike, and eat meat on fast days'.[12]

As well as the diary of Surgeon Superintendent Strutt, we are also lucky to have a record of the voyage of the *Thomas Arbuthnot* written by Sir Arthur Hodgson, described as 'squatter, politician and squire'.[13] He had been educated at Eton and served in the Royal Navy. He emigrated to Sydney in 1839 and after gaining experience on land in New South Wales had taken the risk of moving north and in 1840 took up land at Eton Vale, the second run on the Darling Downs. He met with mixed fortunes there initially due to drought, low prices and transport difficulties but later became very wealthy and in 1858 he won a seat in the New South Wales parliament. He travelled on the *Thomas Arbuthnot* with his wife and child, returning home to Australia.

By Tuesday 30 October, two days out from Plymouth, due to a swell at sea and constant rain, Strutt reported that 'about sixty were seasick'. One can only imagine the terror this must have induced in the girls, being tossed around in their bunks, lying on their straw 'mattresses', the ship rolling in heavy seas, water pouring in through a leaky deck, pitch darkness in their sleeping quarters, the noise of the goods in the hold sliding and banging off each other. Not to mention the pigs, sheep and fowls on board similarly protesting at their accommodation. Strutt immediately thought about the girls and 'went down to console and encourage my people'.[14]

Hodgson reiterates the seasickness on board, which seemed to affect everyone, but by 4 November, he reports that 'the worst part of our voyage may now be considered to be over'.[15] He also tells us on the same day that 'some of our sheep have died, also many of our poultry'.[16]

On the *Thomas Arbuthnot* the surgeon superintendent had the extra duty of organising a school for the girls, and on Sundays it was his duty to preach a sermon and conduct a religious ceremony. He was impartial in his handling of all complaints and when there was 'more noise than was seemly during prayers, I stopped the lime juice of Miss Collins as she would not point out the guilty party'.[17] Miss Collins had been an assistant matron in Listowel Workhouse and she had volunteered to emigrate herself, travelling as an assistant matron on the *Tipoo Saib*.

Mary Moriarty

Mary Moriarty was one of the twenty girls selected in the Dingle Workhouse for emigration to Australia under the Earl Grey Scheme. Her older sister Catherine was also selected. Mary and Catherine were daughters of Maurice Moriarty and Margaret Cahalane. On arrival, Mary is recorded as being 16 years of age, Roman Catholic, able to read, and that both her parents were dead. From extant records in the Presbytery in Dingle, we know now that the correct age for Mary was 17 when she arrived, as she was born in 1833. We can see from her life in Australia that she was feisty, quick and intelligent and would appear to have had a good knowledge of English as well as her native Irish.

Mary spent a short time in the reception centre in Sydney before travelling onwards with Catherine and a number of the other Dingle and Listowel girls to Moreton Bay. She was initially indentured to Thomas Hennessy, Breakfast Creek at £7-£8 per year. Trevor McClaughlin relates Mary's fate with Mr Hennessy:

> When Thomas Hennessy complained to the Brisbane bench that his apprentice, Mary Moriarty, had absented herself from his service and listed her numerous faults and misconduct, Moriarty replied with allegations of sexual harassment: 'Hennessy used to come to the sofa to me every morning and make use of expressions I cannot repeat and because I laughed, he struck me and kicked me down'.
>
> Hennessy's defence that he had to go to the sofa every morning to get her up 'or she'd be there 'till 9 o'clock' was not strong enough to overcome the court's suspicions, and the bench cancelled the agreement and compelled Hennessy to pay Mary wages amounting to £1.2s.8d.

Soon after this, on 9 June 1852, Mary married Samuel J. Brassington in Brisbane, then a part of New South Wales. The witnesses were James Fitzgerald and Catherine Moriarty, both of Brisbane. Samuel would appear to have been a convict, arriving in Moreton Bay on the *Mount Stewart Elphinstone* on 1 June 1849, sentenced to seven years at Stafford Quarter Sessions. His crime was 'larceny of person' or pickpocket. He received his ticket of leave in Moreton Bay in 1849.

We learn something of Mary's life from the *Charleville Times, Brisbane*, written in 1947 when one of her grandsons was the Speaker of the Queensland Legislative Assembly:[18]

> Samuel Brassington and his wife, the Grandparents of the present Speaker of the Queensland Legislative Assembly, Mr. S. J. Brassington,

were among the early settlers of the Upper Warrego River. Mr. Brassington took up *Old Killarney* in 1864 and the couple lived in a bark hut surrounded by a stockade, which afforded protection from the hostile natives. Very often 'Granny' Brassington as she was familiarly known in later years, had a trying time protecting her family and property during the absence of her husband, who found it necessary to go to Ipswich by covered wagon for the necessary supplies to keep his family and others in the locality, going. In 1870, Mr. Brassington acquired Reynella holding from Messrs. Gordon and Flood, who were also the owners of Gowrie station. He held it until 1891, when the lease expired. He also held Bellrose holding from 1881 to 1889, in which year he sold it to Mr. W. Pennaldurick, who died in the Maranoa district, two years ago at the age of 96. When news reached Mrs. Brassington, by bush telegraph, that there was a white woman (Mrs. Mary Janetzky) living at Gowrie Station (Charleville), she rode down the Warrego side-saddle to make her acquaintance and a ripe friendship existed between Mary Brassington and Mary Janetzky thence onwards.

On Saturday 1 April 1916, the *Brisbane Courier* printed an obituary of Mary Moriarty.[19]

PASSING OF A PIONEER
The Late Mrs. Brassington

The death occurred suddenly on St. Patrick's Day of 'Grandmother' Brassington, the oldest Identity on the Warrego, aged 83 years, writes our Augathella correspondent. Deceased enjoyed very good health up to a week previously when she had an attack of dengue fever. She seemed to recover from this and was quite well until St. Patrick's morning when she donned the colours of her native land – about 12 o'clock, she was discovered unconscious and expired without gaining consciousness.

The deceased lady was born in Dingle, County Kerry, Ireland in 1833. Her maiden name was Mary Moriarty. Together with her sister Mrs. Catherine Elliott (who pre-deceased her) she arrived in Australia, in Sydney in 1849 in the ship *Thomas Arbuthnot*, shortly afterwards coming to Queensland where both sisters married. Mrs. Brassington was

Mary Moriarty.

married in the year 1851 and in that year, she and her husband came to the Condamine and started a shoemaker's shop. Next they arrived in Roma [Bona?] and then went into an Hotel at Donnybrook. Selling out the Hotel they arrived on the Warrego River in 1865, where they built the first house (an hotel) at Augathella.

Giving up hotel life Mr. and Mrs. Brassington took over Reynella and Bellrose stations, but owing to had luck and bad seasons this venture did not prove profitable, so they left Reynella and returned to Augathella and opened a store keeping and butchering business.

The deceased lady's husband pre-deceased her 15 years ago, when 'Grandmother' finally retired to Private life. She was known as one of the most generous hearted of women and was dearly loved by all who knew her. She had a family of 4 sons and 7 daughters, of whom 2 sons and 4 daughters are living, together with 69 grandchildren and 52 great-grandchildren. The sons and daughters living are George and Maurice Brassington, Mrs Sarah Ware, Mrs Hannah Creevey, Mrs Margaret Smith (Augathella), and Mrs Bridget Gordon (Morven).

By 1 December, Strutt was recording 'The girls are getting into good habits of cleanliness, order and tidiness and the school is well attended'. On Sunday 4 December, Hodgson reports 'Emigrants washing clothes. They wash twice in the week, Tuesdays and Fridays.'[20]

By 7 December, the girls were now 'my girls'. His diary tells us on that day 'My girls have become much more orderly and tidy under the constant steady pressure I keep up, against holes, rags, tatters, and dirt. They are pretty good as a body.' That week Strutt had to stay up most of the night with Margaret Nelson (Clare) who had a severe epileptic fit, and he also delivered one of the married women passengers with a baby girl.

As well as all his other duties and responsibilities, Strutt was not above doing a bit of cooking if he felt it was called for. On Saturday 17 December as well as making a 'wire grating for the fore hatch' (to prevent unauthorised visits from male passengers) he also had 'made a meat and sago pudding for my sick girls, which was highly approved'.[21]

While Strutt was laying down the law on the standards he required, turning mattresses, fumigating bedding and keeping up pressure on the girls to attend the school, it was not all work and no play. In the evenings on deck, there was much singing and dancing. The girls were also allowed to bring up their 'boxes' from the hold, which always caused great excitement.

On Christmas Day 1849, the *Thomas Arbuthnot* was off the Cape of Good Hope. The captain handed out plum pudding and Strutt made them 'five bucketfuls of punch, by way of cheering their spirits'.[22] This was his way of uplifting their depressed mood after the previous day:

> Yesterday was devoted to keening, that is, to deploring their fate, old Ireland, and their friends and relations. Seven or eight would get together in a little circle, and keep up a most dismal howling ... I dispersed one or two of these clubs and Mrs Murphy routed the rest by giving public notice that the keeners should have no pudding to-day. which proved an effectual remedy for their grief, so they fell to dancing and singing instead.[23]

On 12 January Hodgson records that 'One of the Emigrants, Mary Casey, deprived of speech'.[24] Mary Casey was one of the Listowel girls.

On Monday 4 February, they came into Sydney 'cove' and were immediately visited by the emigration agent, Mr Merriewether, the port doctor and the Anglican clergyman:

> They were greatly pleased with the order and regularity of the ship, the fatness of my girls, and the cleanliness of their berths, tables, deck, pots and pans etc., and to do the poor wretches justice, they deserved the praise, for they had exerted themselves and worked like horses.[25]

On Friday 8 February, the girls were transferred to a steamer to take them into port. Strutt walked at their head to the Hyde Park Barracks, referred to as 'The Depot'. Not before there was 'much weeping and wailing at leaving the ship'. 'I stopped nearly all day at the Depot with them, got them settled as well as I could. They will now be visited by the Catholic clergy and nuns, for about a fortnight, confessed and persuaded to take the pledge. They will then be permitted to take situations'.[26]

In October 1849, Strutt was the subject of a letter to the Land and Colonial Emigration Office from the Australian authorities. It concerned the difficulty the authorities were having in getting surgeon superintendents for the Irish Orphan Emigrants, at the current rate of 10s per emigrant landed alive. The letter reminded the Imperial Government of the extra responsibility involved with the Irish orphans and requested that the gratuity for each orphan landed alive should be 12s 6d. In the case of the *Thomas Arbuthnot*, about to sail, 'A gentleman named Strutt, who has been employed in our service, with much credit to himself, is one to which we think that the increased scale of remuneration might be very properly extended'.[27]

The twenty-five Kenmare girls were next to depart on the *John Knox*, which left Plymouth on 6 December 1849 and, 140 days later, arrived at Port Jackson on 29 April 1850. Doctor Greenup was the surgeon superintendent. His wife, two sons and three daughters also travelled as cabin passengers. From the English Channel to the Cape of Good Hope, they reported experiencing nothing but 'light baffling winds'.[28] They called at the Cape and stayed there eight days as they had trouble with water leaking from the casks on board. They set sail again on 10 March 1850 four days later they spoke to the ship *Earl Grey* on its way to Hobart with female convict prisoners. There were a total of 344 'Government Emigrants', all registered as Irish, on the *John Knox*, including nineteen married couples with their children. There were two births during the voyage, an 18-year-old girl died on 28 January and four infants died later. While the Irish records show the names of twenty-five girls selected, we can account for only twenty-three arriving.

The *John Knox* had on board girls from Cork, Tipperary, Monaghan, Meath, Cavan and Down. The *Sydney Morning Herald* of 30 April 1850 reported that Captain Davidson's ship had imported '30 tons pig iron, 9

Tippoo Saib *logbook*.

tons chains, 176 tons salt, 2000 bushels rock salt, 3cwt sheet copper, 8 barrels oilman's stores, 16 crates earthenware, 52 casks, 17 hogheads, 22 tierces soda ash, 10 bales candlewick, 203 barrels rosin, 81/4 barrels soap, 236 feet pitch pine, 1770 feet deals, 11 cases, 1 truss, Order'.[29]

From the records we know that a number of the girls on the *John Knox* were placed in Sydney, and others, particularly the Kenmare girls, were moved on to Moreton Bay. It is significant to note that these were the girls who couldn't read or write. They were also probably moved on north as they did not have any experience at housekeeping, seamstress or other occupations that the Sydney hires had.

Finally, seventeen girls left Listowel Workhouse and travelled initially to Dublin and on to Plymouth to leave on what was the final 'female orphan' ship to arrive in Sydney – the *Tippoo Saib*. This 1,022-ton ship with Captain Morphew sailed from Plymouth on 8 April 1850. The surgeon super-intendent on board was Dr Church, who travelled with his wife and was allocated a cabin.

As well as the 297 Irish girls there were also a number of families, single women and ten children, six of them under the age of 10.

For the girls on the *Tippoo Saib* the novelty of their new environment soon wore off. While the food supplied was plentiful and of good quality, they suffered from the usual seasickness, partly the result of fear and trepidation of the unknown consequences of a rolling ship, high waves and a dark, cramped living accommodation.

Four months later, following brief stops for supplies and water in Teneriffe and Capetown, the *Tippoo Saib* was escorted into Sydney Harbour on 29 July 1850. Capt. Morphew's report to the health authorities in Sydney stated that, of his passengers, one was suffering from lunacy, one had consumption, and another hysteria, Three had died on the voyage from 'exhaustion, nervous irritation, and infection of the brain'.[30]

The *Freeman's Journal* (Sydney) recorded the *Tippoo Saib* arriving in Sydney on 8 April with 'Passengers: Dr. Church and wife, Mr. Jackson and 249 emigrants'[31]

Overall the Kerry girls on the four ships appear to have had reasonable voyages, were definitely well looked after, in so far as was possible on a crowded nineteenth-century ship. While we don't have any records extant that tell us how the colonial authorities viewed the immigrant ships that brought the Kerry girls to Australia, we have mixed reports on other Irish 'orphan' ships:

Lady Peel 'Likely to be useful in the colony and well behaved during the voyage' Half the Surgeon's gratuity withheld for inefficient performance of his duties.

Lady Kennaway: Irish Orphan Ship. The girls behaved very well on the voyage and the Immigration remarks that very general approbation has been expressed with their character and capabilities.

Pemberton: The ship arrived in a superior state of cleanliness; the arrangements are said to have been highly satisfactory, and the emigrants were grateful for their treatment. The efficiency of the surgeon, Dr. Sullivan, has since led to his receiving a colonial appointment.

New Liverpool: An Irish orphan ship. Immigrants said to be totally uneducated and never to have been in any service. The girls from one Union were extremely refractory and troublesome.

WORKING LIFE AND MARRIAGE IN AUSTRALIA

WHEN THE FIRST of the ships taking the Irish orphans to Australia arrived there in September 1849, the orphans arrived in a country that had only been settled by Europeans sixty-one years previously. Before 1788, Australia was populated by about 300,000 aborigines. These nomadic people had inhabited the world's oldest continent for more than 10,000 years. The aborigines reaction to the arrival of settlers was varied and sometimes hostile, particularly when the colonisers' occupation led to destruction of lands and food resources, in turn leading to starvation, demoralisation and eventually annihilation of their way of life. In 1846 the British Government passed a law that new land leases should not deprive the indigenous people of their rights to hunt over land fenced or cultivated, but on the ground these laws were mostly ignored. A widespread economic depression was experienced by the new settlers between 1841 and 1846 because of drought and the collapse in wool prices. Thousands were bankrupted and there was mass unemployment. However, by 1849 the economy had improved and the colonial government passed a law that would give squatters fourteen-year leases to their runs. This law gave the squatter temporary security and enabled him and his family to clear their land, plant and stock their selections and make plans for the future.

In the Australian cities of Sydney, Melbourne and Adelaide an aspiring middle class was emerging with new ambitions and requirements.

The advertisements in the daily newspapers were offering for sale not only expensive 'Parisian millinery' and 'superior French vinegar' but also 'rosewood pianofortes, and very superior violins'. There were advertisements for silks, satins and velvet bonnets richly trimmed in the latest fashion.[1]

Even in outlying towns there were requests for trained and experienced staff:

> WANTED, a respectable person as Governess for a family in the town of Bathurst, competent to impart a sound English education, with Music and Drawing, references will be required.

> WANTED, for the country, a Governess competent to teach French and Music besides every other branch of a solid Education.[2]

It was a time of great change, unlimited opportunity, but also many dangers in this new world, when the Kerry orphans set foot in Australia.

Unfortunately the selection of the first lot of orphans to arrive from Ireland on the *Roman Emporer* and the *Inconstant* would appear to have been carried out without much attention to the rules prescribed regarding age (14–18 years) and suitability, of the girls for their new lives. Religion also reared its head early on. When the *Roman Emporer* docked in Adelaide in October 1848 with orphans from Belfast, Cookstown, Dungannon and Magherafelt workhouses, a report in the *South Australian Register* tells us that 'This splendid emigrant ship has made a passage of less than three calendar months from England. The orphans were Irish girls from the Union houses of the North of Ireland, and professed Protestants'.[3] The paper continued with its views that the Irish orphan scheme was 'not only a fraud upon the colonists, but as fraught with the most serious evils to the legitimate emigration scheme and to the social and moral interests of the community'.[4] To drive home the message, the paper also reported the views of a British MP who had visited the ship on the eve of her departure: 'They are a rough lot.'[5]

When the second group of Irish orphans arrived on the *Insconstant* on the 7 June 1849, it was the orphans' suitability for the labour market that was criticised. It was reported in a letter from the Children's Apprenticeship

Board to the Colonial Secretary's office 'that only about 35 can milk cows and the remainder show no disposition to learn, many of these also know nothing of washing of clothes'.[6] These reports did not affect the hiring of these first girls, as most of them had been hired within two weeks.

Working life in Australia for the Irish girls arriving was governed by a strict apprenticeship agreement signed by the apprentice and her employer and properly witnessed. Only someone 'qualified by their clergyman' could supposedly hire one of the girls. If a girl was under 18 years of age, 'the engagements must be by indentures ... and those indentures will continue in force until the servant arrives at the age of nineteen'.[7] Those girls aged 18 years and over were to be hired as prescribed by the Hired Servants Act. The rules for payment were: for girls of 14 years and under 15 years were to get £7 per year, between the ages of 15 and under 16 years it would be £8 per year and anyone under 17 years was to get £9 per year. All the girls above 17 years would get £10 per annum. Judging from the contracts entered upon by the Kerry girls, this pay scale was strictly observed by the employers. If one of the girls wanted to get married, permission had to be sought.

To the Irish orphans arriving, this pay rate seemed to be very generous and beyond their wildest dreams, but we know from comparisons with the going rate it was very low. With hindsight, the orphans were not trained so they would have probably merited a lower rate in any case, but when the rate was initially set, the colonial administrators were expecting to get fully trained/experienced domestic staff at cut prices. At the time that this payscale was drawn up, another Irish girl (not one of the Earl Grey girls), Mary McCarthy of Shanagolden, aged 21, was writing home to Lady Monteagle, who had helped large numbers of families to emigrate to the Melbourne area, telling her that she was getting £14 a year as a housemaid and another Monteagle emigrant, Michael Martin, reported 'single women gets from £15 to £20 (with their board).'[8]

Mary Brandon

Mary Brandon was in Listowel Workhouse, and on her departure for Australia, her address was given as Newtownsandes. However, on arrival she herself gave her address in Ireland as Ballylongford. She was aged 16, could read and write and her parents, Thomas and Mary Anne, were 'both dead'. While there are a number of Brandon families in the Tarmons and Ballylongford area, despite an extensive trawl through baptismal records in both Ballylongford and Newtownsandes, County Kerry, from 1829 to 1834, I could not trace Mary's parents or a baptismal certificate.

Mary was again one of the lucky girls who departed on the *Thomas Arbuthnot* from Plymouth on 28 October 1849, arriving in Port Jackson on 3 February 1950. During the voyage, she and the other girls from Listowel and Dingle were under the supervision and care of Surgeon Superintendent Charles Strutt. She was even luckier to be one of the girls who travelled with Surgeon Strutt on the journey to Yass, and he carefully arranged placements for his charges at locations along the way. However, they were only on the road a couple of days when disaster struck. Two of the drays crashed into each other and in the accident, Mary Brandon and Mary Conway (both Listowel girls) were thrown off and the wheel went over their legs. Strutt had no option but to leave the girls behind in Camden, but not before he put them in the care of an Italian priest – Fr Rogers.

Mary's great-great-grandson Neal W. Chiddy relates:

After Mary Brandon and Mary Conway were left behind at Camden in the care of Revd Ruggiero Emanuel or as his name had been anglicised, Father Rogers, both girls were in a state of shock and disbelief at their predicament. After travelling so far and their final destination only a few weeks away, the thought of losing the only friends and people they knew was devastating. True to his word Father Rogers tried his best to calm and settle them down, finding accommodation and care for them both. He visited them regularly and when they were well enough he found positions of employment for them. Mary Conway was in service for a settler at Appin some twenty odd miles from Camden. Mary Brandon's leg had not quite healed so he found a position for her in Camden.

Mary Conway settled in well at Appin and only visited Camden infrequently. She eventually married her settler and they moved from Appin and settled in the Wagga Wagga district. On Sunday 28 of April Dr Strutt visited Mary [Brandon] at Camden. He was returning to Sydney after seeing all his girls were happy and settled in their new homes in the vast Yass district. He found Mary very unhappy; she completely broke down when she first saw him. When she had calmed her down and they had spoken for some time he realised he couldn't leave her without trying to help her. She had told him she wanted to travel to Yass to be with people she knew. He decided that he would travel to Campbelltown and speak with Fr Rogers. A few weeks later Mary, in company with Fr Rogers, was on her way into the Burragorang Valley where she was put into service with an Irish family, Charles and Mary Collins. Both had been convicted to seven years' transportation: Charles in 1835 and Mary [née Donovan] at Tipperary.

Surname: DONOVAN; First name: MARY;
Sex: F; Age: 24; Place of trial: County Tipperary; Date of trial: 27/12/1837; Description of crime: Larceny; Sentence: Transportation 7 yrs.[9]

When our Mary joined the family she was treated more like a daughter than a maid. From the day she arrived until the day Mary Collins died in 1890 whenever Mary (Brandon) needed help she was there. The Catholic Church was not far from the Collins farm which they both attended regularly. It was at this Church where she met Henry Chiddy.

Henry Chiddy was born at St James Parish Bristol 1823, his parents were Henry and Mary, who were married in 1819 and there was a sister born in 1820. Henry's father remarried in 1828 to Mary Ann in St James Bedminster. His mother died sometime between 1823 and 1828. Henry's father died of tuberculosis he may have been infected by nursing his wife. The family was really in trouble; his father, being a stonemason, would have been unable to work.

Henry was arrested on the 5th March 1835 and charged with stealing the goods of Charles Wintle and was ordered to be imprisoned at hard labour for three months. He was released on the 14th of July 1835. He was again arrested on the 19th of November 1835 for stealing candles to the value of 8 pence and was sentenced to transportation for 7 years. His son John said his father always maintained he was innocent of this charge and was sitting on the side of the road when arrested.

Henry was transferred from the local goal onto the hulk *Justitia* and after being examined by a doctor he was transferred onto the convict transport *Lady Kennaway* a short time later. The doctor's report states 'Henry Chiddy age 13 years was in good health and was well behaved'. *The Lady Kennaway* departed Portsmouth on the 11th of June 1836 and on the 12th of October 1836 they entered Sydney Harbour, the next day Henry was transferred to the juvenile prison where new indents noted he was 16 years. Why this was done I think was that it was easier to assign a 16 year old than a 13 year old. Henry was quickly assigned to Patrick Carlon of Irish Town on the outskirts of Sydney. Patrick Carlon had been granted 80 acres of land in Burragorang Valley and he and Henry regularly travelled there to clear land and prepare for the Carlon Family to move down there. Patrick Carlon was Catholic and missed not having a church in the area and so he donated land in order that a church could be built. In 1836 there weren't many people living in upper Burra-gorang but there were enough Catholics and they rallied around to build their church. Henry being a Protestant was encouraged by Patrick Carlon and the visiting Priests to convert to Catholicism and on the 26th of July 1840 at St. John's Church Campbelltown he did so.

On 8 October 1841 Henry was given his Ticket of Leave. A letter from Colonial Secretary's Office states:

Is His Excellency's the Governor's plea-sure to disperse with the attendance government work of Henry Chiddy was tried at Bristol 2nd sessions 4th January

Mary Brandon.

NSW Registry of Births, Deaths and Marriages

Transcription requested by	NEAL	CHIDDY	05-Oct-98

Registration Number	15530
Date of Death	17 DEC 1902
Place of Death	CEDAR CREEK, PICTON
Name	MARY CHIDDY
Occupation	MARRIED WOMAN
Sex	FEMALE
Age	67
Cause of Death	ENTERITIS, CARDIAC FAILURE
Duration	2 DAYS, SOME YEARS
Medical Attendant	L DAVENPORT PARRY, 17 DEC
Father	THOMAS BRANDON
Father's Occupation	NOT KNOWN
Mother - Maiden Name	MARY ENWRIGHT
Informant	ISABELLA CREIGHTON, DAUGHTER, BALMAIN
When Buried	19 DEC 1902
Where	ROMAN CATHOLIC, UPPER PICTON
Undertaker	JOHN WARTERS
Minister	P J BOUGH
Religion	ROMAN CATHOLIC
Witnesses	JAMES CONNELLAN, ALEXANDER SCOTT
Where born	COUNTY KERRY, IRELAND
Time in Colony/State	ABOUT 52 YRS NSW, ABOUT 2 YRS VIC
Place Married	CAMPBELLTOWN NSW
Age at Marriage	16
Spouse	HENRY CHIDDY
Children of Marriage	JOHN 50, MARY 48, ELIZABETH 46, HENRY 44, ANDREW 42, THOMAS 40, ISABELLA 38, STEPHEN A 36, ANNIE 34, CLARA 32, JAMES 30, OWEN P 28 LIVING NONE DECEASED
Other Comments	

This is a transcription and NOT a certified copy from the Registers of Births, Deaths and Marriages and cannot be used in any legal proceedings whatsoever.

JOY MURRIN - *Transcription Agent*
NSW Births, Deaths and Marriages
PO Box 278, Oatley, NSW   2223
Phone (02) 9585-1187 Fax (02) 9585-1486

Left *Mary Brandon Chiddy's death registration, 17 December 1902.*

Below *Mary Brandon's death certificate.*

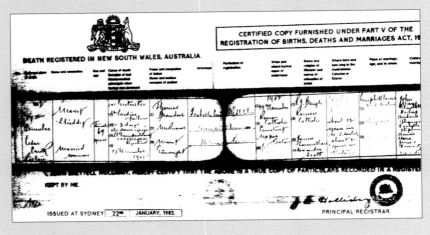

CERTIFIED COPY FURNISHED UNDER PART V OF THE REGISTRATION OF BIRTHS, DEATHS AND MARRIAGES ACT, 19

DEATH REGISTERED IN NEW SOUTH WALES, AUSTRALIA.

ISSUED AT SYDNEY 22ᴺᴰ JANUARY, 1982.

PRINCIPAL REGISTRAR

1836 for seven years arrived per ship *Lady Kennaway* in the year 1836 and to permit him to employ himself (off the stores) in any lawful occupation within the District of Yass for his own advantage during good behaviour.

Henry remained in the Yass district for only for two years and then moved back into Burragorang Valley where he had a lot of friends and he felt at home there:

In 1850 while attending Church at Upper Burragorang he met Mary Brandon and on the 26th of September 1851 they were married in St John's Church Campbelltown. Henry purchased 34 acres of land on a section of the Tonally River know as Tin Kettle Creek and not far from the Church and the Collins family. He built a house and cleared the land, planting fruit trees, some that were still there in the 1950s when the old house was pulled down and the old fruit cut uprooted before it was flooded by the rising waters of the Warragamba Dam. Even though Henry and Mary sold the farm in 1853 it was still known as Chiddy's Farm until the day it was pulled down. They raised eleven healthy children there and as there were no schools Mary taught them the three Rs. She also taught them to play the Fiddle, two of the boys had bands James in Burragorang and my great grandfather Andrew at Thirlmere with his son Brandon.

Henry and Mary moved from their beloved farm at Tin Kettle Creek – I love that name, apparently when the fist explorers went into the valley they found a tin kettle with a large hole in the bottom on the bank of the river – Mary was having heart problems and needed to be closer to a doctor, there weren't any doctors in the valley, so they sold their farm and bought a 120-acre farm at Cedar Creek not far from Picton where there was a Catholic Church. They lived there in semi retirement for the next twenty years.

Mary died on the farm on the 17th December 1902 of Enteritis, and heart failure, and was buried in the Upper Picton Catholic Cemetery. Henry died on the 8th of June 1909 at his daughter Elizabeth's home in Picton and was buried next to Mary in Upper Picton.

The *South Australian Register* reported on the arrival of the *Elgin* with the Killarney girls on board, in 12 September 1849 'The female orphans on board the *Elgin* expressed themselves highly satisfied with their treatment, and the Captain says he has not a fault to find with the young women.'[10] However, over the previous year, partly due to the inbuilt prejudice to girls who had been introduced to their colony from workhouses, partly due to the reports issued in their newspapers warning that the colony would become a receptacle for 'thieves, bastards and prostitutes', the placement of the orphans in suitable employment was very slow. A minority of the girls from the previous two ships had not covered themselves in glory.

There were girls from Skibbereen, Fermoy, Lismore, and Clonmel Unions as well as Killarney among the 190 who arrived in Adelaide on 12 September 1849. Unfortunately any list of names and corresponding workhouses does not survive. We are left with trying to identify the Kerry girls from their names in the Kerry Catholic baptismal records and nineteen girls were provisionally identified. Of these, only three are positive. Mary Healy and Ellen Powell, both from Killarney and Ellen Leary from Glenflesk, have been definitely identified by their descendants. Gayle Dowling, Ellen Powell's great-great-granddaughter visited Ireland and was present in Kilrush at the National Famine Commemoration in May 2013. She collected Ellen's baptismal records from Killarney but was taken aback to find the following written in Latin: '*Idem B: Ellen filiu illegtimus Johannis Powel Heretic & Catherina Flynn de filia.*'

John Powell, Ellen's father, appears to have been an overseer or agent of Lord Kenmare. 'John Powell, was in possession of two properties at Scrahane at the time of Griffith's Valuation. Roseville Cottage, valued at £8 was vacant while the second property was leased to Capt. John Kenny. Bary

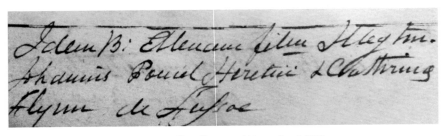

The baptism certificate of Ellen Powell, Killarney, 4 December 1826.

states that the house may have built and used by Lord Kenmare for one of his agents.'[11]

Three days after the *Elgin* arrived at the port of Adelaide, the Office of the Children's Apprenticeship Board, who were responsible for the girls, advertised on Saturday 15 September:

> The *Elgin*, with female orphans, arrived. Applicants desirous of availing themselves of their Services, are requested to attend, in person or by proxy, at the Office of the Secretary, Native School, on and after Friday next, the 14th instant. It is recommended that the orphans be removed immediately after the arrangements have been made. Signed M. MOORHOUSE, Secretary to the Board.[12]

The negative publicity, together with stories of misbehaviour of the girls who had arrived on the two earlier ships, whether true or false, meant an unwelcome environment awaited the *Elgin* group. While a number of them had been moved to the Native School for hiring, some must also have also been kept on board the ship, which delayed its return to London. By 29 December the *Elgin* was still in Port Adelaide awaiting loading. Most of this delay was attributable to the delay in finding places for the orphans.[13]

Further accusations of immoral conduct, 'Bacchanalian orgies' and allegations that the Native School was being run as a 'Government Brothel' were levelled at the orphans while in this Depot, and were in turn refuted by the Children's Apprenticeship Board.

On Saturday 20 October the *South Australian Register* reported on a case where a local farmer had used threatening and abusive language to a publican and was also charged with an assault on Johanna Donovan, one of the *Elgin* girls. Mr J.J. O'Sullivan, who acted as schoolmaster on board the *Elgin*, spoke in Johanna's defence. He said he:

> thought the case too serious to be disposed of summarily, adding that it had been stated in the papers that more than 21 of the Irish orphans were on the town. No wonder, if they were treated as this one had been! His official duties had ceased but he considered himself morally bound to afford the poor girls such protection as was in his power.[14]

Johanna, giving evidence stated that she had arrived on the *Elgin* about three weeks previously.

> A person, whom she could not identify, engaged her at the Depot on the 10inst. Whilst walking with him from the Depot, he told her that he had hired her as a married man, but he was not, and he was going to get rid of the old women he was living with, and he wanted her heart and hand and not her service. She rejected his proposals and said she would not live with him that way as she had nothing but her character to depend on. He replied he had plenty of money and if he did her any harm he would pay her well for it. He offered her some spirits from a bottle he had with him and asked her to unfasten his waistbelt; then he began to pull her about and tried to kiss her.

A witness came along at this point and, taking stock of the situation, took her on to a house where he knew there was another Irish orphan. Her assailant was bound to appear again the following week.[15]

Charles Brewer, immigration agent in Adelaide, replying to a query in the *Register* on the 27 October, said:

> there is not sufficient care taken in their selection, the consequence of which is, that many of them are on the streets of Adelaide. The Irish orphans who came out on the *Elgin*, conducted themselves well on the voyage, and are considered by the Orphan Board to have been more carefully selected than those by the *Roman Emperor* or *Inconstant*, but there is some difficulty in getting them hired, the colony being now much better supplied with a more generally useful class of female servants.

On 10 November, Ellen Walsh, who according to the *South Australian Register* 'came out on the Elgin', was in court accused of stealing £5. The witness in court said that Ellen, having 'left her place, she was allowed to sleep there [in the witnesses' rooms] for the night'.

By August 1850, the Irish orphans were still making headlines. 'Catherine Ryan, an Irish orphan per the *Elgin*, was brought up on remand, charged with stealing a brooch and other articles, the property of her employer, August Fischer. No further evidence was brought forward. She made the following statement:

I know I am guilty of stealing the brooch, and the locket; I have nothing else to say. The clothes are my own; I would not have done it, but I had to sleep by the river side for a night. I tried for a week to get a place at Mr Schlesinger's office and could not get one.[16]

The same newspaper on the same page reported:

Mr Morris, keeper of the Lunatic Asylum, brought up an Irish orphan who had been committed to his care, and handed her over recovered to Mr Moorhouse, Secretary to the Orphan Board.[17]

It is hard to know where the truth lay but it is obvious from all the inquiries held by the different parties that the girls who arrived on the *Elgin* were not properly supervised in the native school, their prospective employers were not vetted and where there was a disagreement between employer and employee, the employee had no home or no alternative employment offered to her. Any fair-minded reader would say that they were more sinned against than sinners.

An entirely different picture emerges on the hiring of the girls from the *Thomas Arbuthnot*. All the girls were initially lodged in Hyde Park Barracks, Macquarie Street, originally built to house convict males, and it was from here that interested parties could come to hire the girls. One week after the arrival of the *Thomas Arbuthnot* two of the girls had already been hired. Mr Meriewether, the Emigration Agent, decided to send a number of the girls on into the interior towards Goulbourn and Yass where there were now a number of settlements and stations who would, no doubt, require labour as a result. Charles Strutt, who had been their surgeon superintendent on the ship, offered immediately to go with them and see them into employment. He asked for volunteers and '130 expressed a wish to go to anyplace that I might be going to'.[18] The girls had been cooped up with nuns in the barracks since they arrived and Strutt perceived a 'gloomy, quiet and silent atmosphere'.[19] He felt that the girls had enough praying and wanted to get going to the country.

We believe that at least eight Listowel girls and nine of the Dingle girls went on this further journey with Strutt.

Eventually 108 girls, with at least three matrons (Miss Collins of Listowel and others unnamed), left the barracks and went by steamer to Paramatta, where they lodged that night in the former convict barracks. The following day, Tuesday 19 February, they set out on their journey in fourteen drays drawn by a team of horses. Strutt continued to keep his diary, recording the minutiae of the days as they travelled along the rutted track which was then the forerunner of what was later the Hume Highway. The girls slept outdoors in the bush in makeshift tents with the matrons, subject to insect bites, with parrots, magpies, and cockatoos overhead to wake them early in the mornings. Strutt slept under a dray with the men and drovers and was 'much tormented by ants, fleese [sic] or some such creatures that bit like fury'.[20] He helped to cook and serve their food, meat, potatoes and tea as they travelled. Rations were picked up every few days at stops along the road. 'Little water to be found, and that not good, and far apart.'[21]

They were only on the road two days when disaster struck. Two of the drays crashed into each other and in the melee, Mary Brandon and Mary Conway (both Listowel girls) were thrown off and the wheel went over their legs. Strutt had no option but to leave them at Camden where the accident occurred, under the care of a surgeon magistrate whom he judged to be 'rough and uncouth'.[22] The two Mary's were heartbroken at being left behind, shocked after the accident and now parted from their friends and colleagues with whom they had shared their lives for the previous four months. However, an Italian priest who witnessed the accident guaranteed Strutt that he would look out for them and that they would be well cared for. The very next day, having stopped for the night, Strutt recorded in his diary 'Thurs 21st Stopped for the night at the Haunted Hut, wrote a letter to my two girls'.[23]

On Saturday the 23 February, they approached their first signs of civilisation – Berrima, where the girls got their first sight of 'blacks' as Aborigines are referred to at this time. 'A tribe of blacks were encamped there and frightened the girls'.[24] Goulbourn he found a 'dull, quiet place, with perhaps a 1000 people, two churches, a catholic chapel, a Methodist chapel, a large gaol, a courthouse and several inns'.[25]

On Thursday 1 March, they camped by the river near the home of Hamilton Hume, who was the first to cross the country from Sydney to Melbourne (Port Philip). They were about to enter Yass, where the first hirings would take place, so they took out their boxes here – the boxes they had brought 10,000 miles from Ireland, to dress up and make themselves smart. A number of girls were hired in Yass, but when Strutt discovered the following day that two had been hired by 'improper persons', he promptly took them away. He also had a number of offers of marriage. A 'watchmaker in the town wishes to have a wife, and has consulted me on the subject. He has taken a fancy to one of our matrons, but the affair will be rather difficult'.[26] Another applicant – 'a certain Michael Flynn'[27] – made no bones about it and said he was looking for a wife. 'In five minutes he had selected one'. But this girl was not to be tempted so easily – having given him a false name, she 'quizzed him very much'. Having discovered he was a Ticket of Leave man, and had no money, Strutt sent him to get signatures from the priest and magistrate before proceeding any farther. Strutt comments 'he seemed quite surprised at the difficulty, imagining that he had nothing to do but come and take away any girl he might honour with his choice'.[28]

By Saturday 16 March, forty girls and two matrons had been hired in 'decent places' in the Yass district. It was arranged that another fifteen would stay on there for future placement and Strutt would take the remaining forty-five on to Gundagai. After a tough journey over rough ground, creeks and hills by the Murambidgee river, they reached Gundagai, then a small 'town' of 250 people, with a mail car twice a week to Port Philip and Sydney. By Saturday 23 March, he had hired out eighteen girls of those he took to Yass.

> Some blacks were walking about the town to the great wonderment of the girls – they were a stout limbed race, with nothing but a blanket about them. One had a boomerang ... there are about 200 blacks in the neighbourhood, and about 2000 in the district.[29]

He describes how an aborigine man came into the yard of the barracks and one of the policemen asked him jokingly if he wanted a wife. The man said 'no', he had three already and they would be jealous. The policeman pointed out Biddy and asked if he would have her. 'No' said he with an unmistakable expression of disgust, as if he was on the point of being sick, 'too much yabber'.[30]

Strutt, although he had planned to go on to Allbury, Wagga Wagga and Tumut, where he reasoned that the rest of the girls would be hired, found that there was no need, the last of them were placed in Tumut. He then sold his horse and returned to Sydney by the mail coach, calling on the way at a number of the homes where he had placed girls. In a couple of these he was not satisfied with the hirers and he removed the girls and got new places for them with 'more Christian people'.[31] He stopped off at Camden to check on Mary Brandon and Mary Conway. Mary Brandon, who had recovered but whose leg was still not quite better, had got a satisfactory placement but he wasn't able to see Mary Conway as she lived some miles outside the town. He also got an opportunity to thank the Italian priest for looking after them.

On his return through Yass, Strutt was presented with an address, signed by H. O'Brien, the Warden of the District of Yass and several highly respected citizens, 'expressing the general satisfaction my girls had given in Yass and the neighbourhood'.[32] He mentions at this point that Miss Collins had been placed in a country district outside of Yass. On his return to Sydney, Strutt was thanked in a letter from the Committee. On May 8 he boarded the *Thomas Arbuthnot* and set sail again for England.

While these *Thomas Arbuthnot* girls were placed in widely spread outlying areas of New South Wales, there was some comfort to be had in knowing that groups of them had got placed in the immediate environs of centres such as Yass, Gundagai and Tumut, where we would hope they met in later life.

The girls from Kenmare, who arrived on the *John Knox* in Port Jackson on the 29 April 1850, included inmates of workhouses in Monaghan, Wexford, Tipperary, Down, Cork, Meath and Kenmare. A number of these girls were hired in Sydney, in the outlying areas of Bathhurst and again a number were sent on to Moreton Bay and from thence to Ipswich where they settled and married. Anne Husband of Kenmare was apprenticed to Dr Richard Greenup, who had been the surgeon superintendent on the *John Knox* and who travelled with his wife and children. Dr Greenup initially opened a private practice in Sydney. He was quickly involved in helping to organise the new University of Sydney, became its secretary on 17 March 1851 and later was also treasurer and registrar.

The *Tippoo Saib* was the last ship that left Plymouth to bring orphans to Sydney under the Earl Grey Scheme. It arrived in Sydney on 29 July 1850 with immigrants from Listowel, Limerick, Longford, Meath Leitrim,

Queen's, King's, Westmeath. Unfortunately these Listowel girls did not have the same good luck as their predecessors on the *Thomas Arbuthnot*. From the records that have survived, there is very little information available to us to identify where they got employment. We know that a number were hired immediately in Sydney, two of those being the Listowel Workhouse girls – Julia Daly (Tralee) and Mary Connor (Causeway) who were placed with the solicitor, Mr McCullagh, in Elizabeth Street, but who ran away and were subsequently the subject of a court case. The immigration authorities at Hyde Park prosecuted the case, under the Hired Servants Act, against Captain Morphew of the *Tipoo Saib* who was accused of enticing Julia to run away and live as his wife. He was convicted in his absence, Mary Connor gave evidence for the prosecution and also said that when Julia decided to leave Mr McCullagh, she [Mary] would 'go anywhere with her rather than stop alone'.[33]

The majority of the *Tippoo Saib* girls seem to have been sent on to Moreton Bay again for settlement in the Brisbane and Ipswich areas, in order to dissipate the criticism that was being loudly expressed in the newspapers, principally the *Sydney Morning Herald* and the *Melbourne Argus*, for some time prior to their leaving Ireland in December 1849.

Even before these girls were ever selected from the Listowel Workhouse, hostility to the entire scheme had built up in the colony to such an extent that it was decided to scrap it entirely. In early 1850 a dispatch was on its way to the Colonial Office from Governor Fitzroy, recommending the cessation of this type of emigration. Before the dispatch reached England, four more ships had been sent out, three to Sydney and one to Port Philip.

By September 1850 all the Kerry girls had been placed and were spread throughout South Australia, New South Wales and the vast territory later named as the State of Queensland. By 1853, from Adelaide and Victoria in the south to the Condamine in the North and from the coastal settlements on the Pacific through to the newly explored interior the Kerry girls were living, working and starting to rear families.

Once settled in employment, the vast majority of the Kerry girls were married within a year or two. They mostly married older men who had been in the colony for a number of years, as squatters, stockmen or convicts. The latter now had almost all acquired their Tickets of Leave and were free to move to and from the different districts. In New South Wales and inland from Moreton Bay, the town of Brisbane was opening up and the rapidly developing rich grazing and farming lands in the interior were being settled. These areas attracted immigrants and ex-convicts who were rough and ready to take on the challenges of opening up a new country, taking opportunities or dealing with catastrophes and adversity with the same attitude.

The Kerry girls who went to Moreton Bay and became the female pioneers in the inner unexplored tracts, were to face many of the same challenges when married as they would have had at home. Coming with the experiences which they had from their lives so far in Ireland, these situations were not new to them. The challenges were different in the sense that the physical land that they occupied faced droughts, floods, unusual crops, strange animals and insects, but poverty, hard work, large families, violent and unexpected deaths were all situations with which they were only too familiar. Situations for which they would not have been prepared would be the isolation and monotony of life in the bush, the huge distances from neighbours or help in an emergency. The Kerry girls would not have had any experience of riding horses; here, in their new life, that was the mode of transport expected of them. That is the way they would travel to the nearest habitation or station to get help in a crisis.

If food was plentiful, there were still problems. To keep meat fresh it was generally salted, eating this seven days a week demanded improvisation and imagination. Later, when life got somewhat easier, they kept chickens and pigs. Those near to the great Australian rivers like the Manning River in northern New South Wales would have had a slightly more varied diet: 'Salt Beef was the normal meat, Fowls were reared, pigeons, turkey and fish were plentiful'.[34] Their slab and bark huts would have been a great improvement on the cabins they had left behind, and as the years passed, these were enhanced and extended on their own land without reference to landlord or middleman.

From the descendant's stories and histories of the girls, we know that many of them went to the goldfields with their new husbands. After gold was found in Bathurst in 1851, life changed for ever in Australia. Within a month, thousands were making their way to the goldfields. Later discoveries of gold in Victoria meant that long treks were made on foot, on horseback or by dray to get to the mining localities of Beechworth,

Bendigo and Ballarat. We have many stories of the girls accompanying their husbands on these long trudges, hoping to seek their fortunes at the other end. They lived a nomadic existence in these locations. Initially living in tents where up to 40,000 people could be camped close together, as they were at Bendigo, with all the deprivations of living cheek by jowl with so many others, little or no sanitation, shortages of water, the orphans had to fall back on all the resources they possessed. Food had to be found and cooked. Like the early squatters, miners lived on bread, tea and mutton. As well as cooking, their lot was to chop wood for the fires, washing and helping in the never ending search for the elusive gold. There was a lot of sickness on the diggings, the results of poor living conditions, bad food, heavy manual work and long hours working outdoors in all kinds of weather from the searing heat to downpours and floods. Those who stayed on for a number of years and presumably found some traces of gold, bettered their situation by building slab and bark huts, the wives found other work in the many stores that had sprung up or taking in washing. They kept a few hens and goats, started families and life began to regularise.

Some parents sent their children to school on the diggings. The children's parents paid a fee so that their children could get the education that they had not been able to get themselves. As one could imagine, the standard of education from these schools was not very high. Children moved from one goldfield to another. If there was no teacher there, they had to wait until one turned up. Teachers, like others on the goldfields, lived in tents.[35]

The poor education that the Kerry girls had received prior to their arrival in Australia militated against them in their new homes with their growing children. Those who did not live in the cities and who settled in the bush or the goldfields, in the early years, lived too far away from schools that existed at that time. The fathers, who might have had the basics of reading and writing, after long days of physical work would have little interest or energy to teach their children, and the mothers were unable to do so. 'If a mother on a station or farm could not instruct her children, education was rarely possible and though some older children may have helped the younger ones, few would have had any formal assistance.'[36] Unfortunately we have proof, that some of the first generation of children were still signing their own marriage registers with an 'X'.

We can see that while none of the orphans achieved huge material success, they enjoyed moderate prosperity and it was as one generation succeeded another that their descendants prospered. We learn from the stories of their early times in the colony that in their search for financial security, land or gold they were not successful. In their constant quest for work which would provide them with this security, they uprooted themselves and their families and moved about a lot. 'We are reminded that pioneering required plenty of honest perspiration and unglamorous toil: it also requires a quality of silent heroism and the capacity to endure heartbreak.'[37]

The great difference between the lives of the Kerry girls and their husbands with those of the Limerick Monteagle immigrants was not where they came from, their ages or capacity for hard work. It was that Monteagle emigrants travelled to Australia in family groups; the small amounts of capital that the Limerick people brought and most importantly the chain migration which followed very quickly, was their key to early success. Brothers, sister, cousins and in-laws arrived over the next twenty years, all rowed in to help each other to get jobs and to work, just as they had at home, in the traditional *meitheal*, on each other's farms and stations. Because of this family support, the Monteagle immigrants were very successful almost immediately, acquiring land selections, opening stores in the principal streets of Melbourne, building Hotels on the Hume Highway.

We have no evidence to show that the Kerry girls ever had the opportunity to send home for any of their families or indeed if they even kept in touch with home. A majority of them had lost both their parents and their siblings in the Famine and the link had broken for ever. In one case, that of Ellen Leary, we know that she must have kept in touch with her family in Glenflesk, as three generations later her family were able to say that her brother Ignatius had been ordained as a priest.

Ellen Wilson

Ellen Wilson was aged 19 when she left Listowel Workhouse and sailed on the *Thomas Arbuthnot* from Plymouth on 28 October 1849. Her sister Mary is also recorded as sailing at the same time. On arrival in Sydney it is recorded that both could read and write and were members of the Church of England. No records exist of births for either of these girls in any of the Kerry registers.

They were some of the lucky girls who had travelled with Surgeon Superintendent Strutt, but it is unusual that both were then sent on from Hyde Park Barracks to Moreton Bay. We don't know if they were offered the opportunity to go with Strutt and the other *Thomas Arbuthnot* girls on the journey to Yass.

Ellen was apprenticed to an 'A. Brown' of Brisbane at £8 for one year. Her sister Mary was also employed by the same man on the same conditions. A young Scottish cuddy boy, James Porter, described the orphans who came to Moreton Bay at the end of 1849 being 'treated more like criminals than objects of pity. There [*sic*] hair had been cut short and the blackfellow when he saw them for the first time called them "short grass" consequently they were afterwards called "short grasses".'

Porter's account is invaluable in evoking a picture of the rough masculine society into which the young women were thrown.[38]

We are indebted to Ellen's descendant Brian Grant for the continued story of her life:

Ellen was a resourceful girl and within four or five years of arrival we find her on the Victorian Goldfields, a distance of 1000 miles from Brisbane. She met and married a Kerryman – John Brick in Castlemaine, Victoria in 1856. The priest who signed the Register is called Fr. Barrett. Maybe another Kerryman?

John and Ellen had a child – John Brick (Jnr), in 1861, who is my ancestor, as well as at least six other children – Jeremiah, William, John, Mary, Hanora and Edward. John Brick (Jnr) married the daughter of another Irish Famine 'orphan', Margaret Manning who came on the *Lismoyne*. The family were living in South Melbourne by 1890. One of Ellen's grandsons (John Grant's Grandfather) served in World War 1 with the Australian Army.

Brian Grant also tells us that each descendant family had a number of children and that there are Brick descendants scattered around Melbourne, with a branch in Sydney.

We also have a Catholic priest in the family that my mother was so proud of. His name is Wayne Stanhope. Up until recently he was the head of the Carmelite order in Australia and a great-great-grandson of Ellen Wilson.

For Ellen to get from Moreton Bay to the Victorian goldfields displays her spirit of adventure, her courage and resourcefulness in living in this challenging environment. When gold fever gripped Australia in 1851 it engendered such excitement that men of all sorts threw up their jobs, left their families and took off to seek their fortunes. It was unusual though for a woman to do the same, perhaps Ellen had already met John Brick. The diggers who arrived in Ballarat, Bendigo and Castlemaine came from all walks of life and from countries all over the world.

During the greatest excitement, the rough roads to the diggings were crowded with people – some walking, some on horseback, some pushing wheel-barrows and some with bullock waggons.[39]

The wedding of Ellen and John's daughter, Mary.

Ellen's previous life in famine-stricken north Kerry in Listowel Workhouse, her three-month voyage on the *Thomas Arbuthnot* and her short apprenticeship in Moreton Bay prepared her well for the 1,000-mile trek and her subsequent years at the diggings:

> The digger's residence was commonly a small calico tent on the slopes of the gully where the claim was, and the area occupied by it was twelve by eight. There were many canvas tents and a few log huts and some had rude chimneys. The furniture consisted of one or two stumps of trees for chairs, while anything in the shape of a box or tea chest served for a table. The bed consisted of a stretcher or bunk made of forked stakes and saplings covered with a rug and a pair or two of blankets.[40]

Most of the men digging were strong, self-reliant, hardworking people who hoped the finding of gold, even any small amount, would help them to better their lives.

Brian Grant says of Ellen and John Brick's adventure in Castlemaine, that 'The Bricks couldn't have made a lot from the goldfields, because all their descendants that I know are working class, they didn't leave a nest egg unfortunately'.

However, they settled peacefully in Melbourne, where there was a lot of wealth and employment built on the back of the goldrush and brought up a hard-working family of proud Australian citizens.

Ellen died in Brunswick, Melbourne on 23 September 1894 from acute bronchitis. Her death certificate states that she was born in 'Listowell [*sic*], Co. Kerry, Ireland' and that she was forty years in Victoria. She was 64 years of age.

8

PAWNS IN
AN IMPERIAL STRUGGLE?

W ERE THESE IRISH orphan girls pawns in a political strug-
gle between Imperial and Colonial interests? Or were they
'useless trollops' with low moral standards, as accused by the
Australian newspapers of the day?

Queen Victoria's Empire was at the height of its power. The colonies in
Australia, New South Wales, Victoria, Queensland and Van Diemen's Land
were agitating for self-government which was granted by Earl Grey, in his
capacity as Colonial Secretary, in 1852. Australia was a valuable resource
of wheat, gold and wool to the British Empire. On the other hand their 'Irish
Colony' was troublesome and financially draining. In the forty years that
followed the union, successive British governments grappled with the problems of governing a country which had, as Benjamin Disraeli put it in 1844,
'a starving population, an absentee aristocracy, and an alien Church, and in
addition the weakest executive in the world'.[1] Cecil Woodham-Smith records
that between 1801 and 1845, there had been 114 commissions and sixty-
one special committees inquiring into the state of Ireland and that:

> without exception their findings prophesied disaster; Ireland was on the
> verge of starvation, her population rapidly increasing, three-quarters of her
> labourers unemployed, housing conditions appalling and the standard of
> living unbelievably low.[2]

We can understand how seeing a neat political fix to a situation appealed to Earl Grey and his civil servants in the Colonial Office. Supplying females who would initially fill some of the vacancies that the colonists were desperate for, leading on to marriage with the male surplus, and emptying the workhouses in Ireland of the same females who were costing the ratepayers vast and seemingly unending amounts of money, seemed a no-brainer.

There is no doubt that the girls 'selected' from the workhouses were not qualified or experienced in any way for going 'into service' either for the matrons of Sydney, Melbourne and Adelaide or their compatriots in the outback and the bush. The girls had come in the main from very disadvantaged backgrounds. They would have had absolutely no knowledge of housekeeping and only very little experience of farm work. At home or in the workhouse, they would not have grown crops, fed and cared for cows, sheep or pigs. Prior to their selection and departure, a year or two years living in the workhouse would not have qualified anyone for a life of service in the outside world. Added to these difficulties was their lack of education. We know that the majority of the girls arriving could 'not read or write' according to their arrival records. This may have meant 'could not read or write *English*' as Irish was their first, and in the case of the Dingle and some of the Kenmare girls their only, language. In any, case their English reading and writing would have been poor. It was too soon for the recently established National Schools, set up in 1838 in Ireland to have imparted these skills to this particular set of girls.

An upwardly mobile Australian middle class, particularly in the cities, were now looking for trained staff, those who had previous experience in upper-class homes as housekeepers, cooks, dealing with visitors, educating children and other domestic duties that would pertain in a great house. These girls were also expected to 'know their place', and that was one thing they didn't know – they had spirit, fire and strong personalities, seen as insolence and impertinence by their employers.

Taking into account the disadvantages of their level of service experience, was the furore aroused in the Australian newspapers justified or were there a deeper political agenda at work in which the girls were unwitting pawns?

Mary (Maria) Conway, Listowel

Mary Conway's address on the Minutes of the Listowel Board of Guardians on 11 September 1849 was Dromkeen, Causeway. She had a sad life from her initial accident, through the death of four of her children to her eventual death at the age of 44.

Patricia McGill, great-granddaughter of Mary, tells us her tragic story:

Mary Conway arrived on the *Thomas Arbuthnot* and in February 1850. She was one of a group of girls under the charge of Dr Strutt the Surgeon General on the ship, who were travelling inland for the purpose of being placed in service in the Yass-Gundagai area of New South Wales. When they were passing through the village of Camden west of Sydney, Mary and another girl, Mary Brandon were involved in an accident.

The two girls were unable to travel any further and after receiving treatment for their injuries, were left in the care of a Catholic priest. Following recovery, Mary returned to Sydney and on 1 August 1851, she married Benjamin Castle at St Mary's Church in Sydney. For a period of time after the marriage the couple lived in Castlereagh Street Sydney. Benjamin was an English convict who had been transported in 1837 for housebreaking. He received his ticket of leave in 1844 and Conditional Pardon in 1847. As far as can be ascertained through official records, Mary and Benjamin had six children but only two survived until adulthood.

Between 1858 and 1859, the family was living in Glebe, an inner west suburb of Sydney. In 1860, at the time of Anastasia's death, the family had moved west of Sydney to Picton, a small village. In 1862, when Joseph was born, the family was living at the Old Goulburn township which is further west of Picton.

Nothing further is known of their place of residence until 1876 when it has been established that the family was living in the vicinity of Wagga Wagga in the Riverina district of New South Wales where Benjamin held a farming lease on the Eunonyhareenyma pastoral run.

Mary died in a cart accident on 24 June 1876. She was a passenger in a horse-drawn spring cart driven by her husband Benjamin Castle. They were returning home to Eunonyhareenyma. Approximately five miles from Wagga Wagga the cart overturned and Mary was killed.

At the time of her death, Mary had two surviving children, James and Benjamin. Both of these children reached adulthood. James died on 23 September 1930, aged 76 years and is buried in Rookwood cemetery in Sydney. Benjamin was fatally wounded in a horse and sulky accident in October, 1935 near West Wyalong and is buried in the West Wyalong cemetery. Mary's husband Benjamin died in 1892 and is buried in the Wagga Wagga cemetery.

I am a descendant of Mary's son, Benjamin through my mother, Amy who was his 3rd daughter from his second marriage. She was a grand-daughter of Mary Conway.

It seems that Mary's life had its sad parts with the loss of so many of her children and meeting an untimely death herself. However, her descendants are many and her existence is commemorated on the Memorial which has been erected at the Hyde Park Barracks in Sydney. When I look back over the distance of time, I imagine her to be a strong, courageous young woman who was prepared to face the unknown in this distant, foreign place and make the very best of the conditions for herself and her family. I am very proud to be her descendant.

The negative press and comments started almost immediately after the arrival of the first of the Irish orphans. On Wednesday 13 March 1850, a month before the arrival of the Kenmare girls on the *John Knox*, both an editorial and a series of reports were carried in the *South Australian Register* quoting from other newspapers in the colony – *Sydney Morning Herald*, *Melbourne Morning Herald*, *Goulbourn Herald* and *Melboure Argus* – all containing negative and inflammatory comments on the Irish orphans.[3]

The editorial prefaced its comments by saying that it had not stopped to enquire whether the immigration of the orphans was the work of Caroline Chisholm 'as Dr. Lang alleges', and went on to print in heavy ink:

> We feel sure that we are expressing the universal voice of the public in declaring the present system of Irish female orphan immigration a serious injury to the community, and a wonton abuse of the funds intended by the colonists to procure the immigration of virtuous and reputable parties.[4]

Then, over the rest of the page, it quoted similar articles in other Australian newspapers. The initial paragraphs were stories of unsatisfactory apprentices. In all cases the girls accused of the various misdemeanours denied the accusations. A Mrs Kennedy of Paramatta accused 'Frances Tearnan, an Irish Orphan girl' of being 'impudent in the extreme, and had informed her [Mrs Kennedy] that she would not stand at the wash tub unless she was allowed to wear patent leather shoes'.

Another lady, a Mrs Bennett of Sydney, was quoted before a magistrate as accusing her apprentice of being 'insolent, idle, used bad language, kept bad company and beat the children' and she asked for her indenture to be cancelled. The report went on from there to describe in the most negative terms the structure of the scheme and worked up to a diatribe against Catholicism and its dangers:

> We fear that time will prove that these girls are about the worst class of emigrants that could be sent to the colony ... A gentleman of our acquaintance went yesterday to the Immigrant Barracks to engage an Irish Orphan, at the usual rate of wages, but not one of the whole lot could he procure, because he lived at Brighton [then an outlying country area outside Melbourne]. These girls seem to have got it into their heads that they have come here for the sole purpose of getting married, and that Melbourne consequently holds out greater inducements in that respect than Brighton. Really, we trust that the Government will interfere and bring these young ladies to their senses.

In a more sardonic tone 'There is a kind of liberality which is very profitable – it is making a free gift to others of what has become burdensome to ourselves. England is very prodigal of such presents, her bounty scarcely knows a limit'. The article goes on to say of the Imperial Government: 'If the colonies could only be brought to accept it, she would shift from her own shoulders the entire bulk of her convict and pauper population, and deposit them on the shores of New South Wales.'

But the longest and last contribution is devoted to religion and the perceived problems that will arise from the orphan scheme. The *Melbourne Argus*, always the most negative, states that the time has come to stop this type of emigration before it is 'productive of very serious results'.

In a nutshell, spending our own money, we have a right to expect the very best class of immigrants that can be induced to venture to this happy land, and it is downright robbery to withhold our funds from decent, eligible, well brought up girls, who would make good servants to-day and virtuous intelligent wives to-morrow, than lavish it upon a set of ignorant creatures, whose whole knowledge of household duty, barely reaches to distinguishing the inside from the outside of a potato, and whose chief employment hitherto, has consisted of some such intellectual occupation as occasionally trotting across a bog to fetch back a runaway pig.

Finally:

These women, all Roman Catholics, will naturally wed with our shepherds, hutkeepers, stockmen etc., who as a body we blush to say, are little better than heathens ... The result of such a match, is if the children have any religion at all, they will be Roman Catholics; to an individual; the mother will dictate the religion and some day every one of these girls will be the centre of a Roman Catholic centre.[5]

We stand upon no ceremony when we assert that we should look with very deep grief and dread upon the probability of the majority of our community ever being composed of Roman Catholics.[6]

The most suitable emigrants, from the colonists' point of view, would have been English females, free settlers, not out of orphanages, workhouses or convicts. This expectation was unrealistic, as these types of girls had no wish to travel halfway across the world to a place they regarded as only just above savage. 'But the vision of an Anglo-Saxon Protestant Australia was powerful indeed, and each boatload of Irish was further reminder that this dream was receding, that the mixture was being further diluted.'[7] Charles Trevelyan's warning to Lord Clarendon in 1848 proved correct.[8]

Four years after the last of the 'orphan' ships, in a more thoughtful article on the Labour Question, the *South Australian Register* said:

> They did not want Irish orphans. They wanted shepherds. Some persons might want housemaids, but the great want of labour in the colony was the want of shepherds. But he (the Attorney-General) had ascertained that from the hon. member's district of Moreton Bay, where the best of the Irish orphans had not been sent, that they had all turned out well ; that in life, and that the others had conducted themselves in a creditable manner. He knew that when they first came into the colony the nature of the work might be for awhile strange to them; but scattered as they now were throughout the colony, he could assert, as a class, the Irish orphans had turned out well.[9]

The newspaper and court reports from Moreton Bay reflect different types of accusations and offences to those of Sydney or Adelaide. They were mostly either the employer or the employee requesting that their Indenture be cancelled and both sides giving evidence of why this request should be granted. The girls were mainly accused of 'impertinence' or 'insolence' to their employers and in extreme cases of absconding without notice. On the girls' part, they cited cases of excessive hard work, religious discrimination and impropriety on the part of the employers. The evidence of the girls and their presentation of this evidence shows that there were well able to defend their rights and their characters and did not intend to be subservient to anyone. Margaret Stack was accused by her employer of 'repeated insolence and neglect of duty'. Charles Windmell, her employer, giving evidence, swore:

> I ordered the girl to clean the knives and boots and shoes – it is a general rule in my house to have this done Saturday. I took my boots to her. On Sunday morning I found the knives and boots were not cleaned. I asked her the reason – and she wanted to know what sort of quality we were going to have that we wanted clean knives. I told her that if she didn't clean them Saturday she should Sunday – she said she wasn't going to clean knives or boots or shoes.[10]

Reading the Australian newspapers of the day, there is no doubt that there was an inbuilt prejudice against both Irish females and their Catholic religion. The longer that the colony got settled and began to have confidence in its long-term future the more the wish was to have a replica of the 'mother country'. Old fears and suspicions brought to the colony by English Protestants and Scottish Presbyterians in the main, came to the fore. A number of Ulster Scots, as they liked to be known, had taken their Presbyterian faith with them from the northern counties of Ireland. They had left small farms in Ulster and were now settled as substantial landowners in Australia, and they did not want to find themselves back with a Catholic majority. The difficulties of 700 years of Anglo-Irish relationships had followed to the other side of the world. These fears resulted in discrimination against the Irish population in the colony and the orphans were easy targets. As well as the strident editorials and letters to the main newspapers, James Dunmore Lang, who had protested even before they arrived, now got into his stride. He led a tireless crusade against 'Popery' and the Irish saying that they were 'the most ignorant, the most superstitious and the very lowest in the scale of European civilisation'

In hindsight, Lang had little to fear as a great numbers of the orphans married outside their faith and their large families were latter pillars of the different Christian Churches. Nineteen per cent of the 1,285 orphans who disembarked at Port Phillip were Protestant and 28 per cent were born in the nine counties of Ulster, but they were all labelled with the 'Irish orphan' stigma.[11]

So while the early colonial government wanted to promote family life within a stable society, in reality they wanted this to be a microcosm of what they had left behind in Britain – Victorian values in a white protestant community.

The 'orphan' apprenticeship contracts became another political issue. While the strict structure of indenture or apprenticeship which in the main was adhered to, with recognised rates of pay of between £6 and £8 per year, the rates were actually lower than the current rates then being paid to female servants in the colony. There was a fear that this would have the effect of reducing the wages of *all* female servants.

There is no doubt that the Earl Grey Scheme was meticulously planned and executed. The orphans were well looked after and properly fitted out for their new lives. But they were after all very young and inexperienced girls, sent to the other side of the world with little or no preparation for a new life there. Where they were guided and supported, as they were by Charles Strutt, they thrived. Where they were thrown on their own devices without support, they were not always successful.

The colonial pressure brought the Earl Grey Scheme to an end barely two years after it started. Gold had been discovered in Australia, Britain did not want to lose control of what was now a valuable colony rather than a penal outpost. Considerable profits were being made from the different agricultural exports. British companies as well as individuals were investing in both bush and town. British banks and mortgage companies had by now set up to operate in Australia. By the 1830s, wool had overtaken whale oil as the colony's most important export, and by 1850 New South Wales had displaced Germany as the main overseas supplier to British industry.[12] The Australians who had been paying the bills to bring the immigrants to their shores, made it clear that this would no longer be the case. The Colonial Office in London soon saw the way the political will was blowing and needed no further persuasion to drop the initiative. They had got rid of just over 4,000 workhouse inmates, who would have been a continuing cost on their local ratepayers, without any cost to the Treasury.

Mary Ann Connor

Bev Cook tells us Mary Ann's story:

Mary Anne Connor was my great-great-grandmother, through her youngest daughter Eliza Jane Smith.

Mary Ann was baptised in Kenmare on 21 March 1832, the daughter of Edmund (Edward) Fitzgerald and Mary O'Connor at the Church of the Holy Cross. Her parents may not have been married as she was baptised as Mary Fitzgerald but then went by her mother's name of Connor. Her Sponsor was Mary Fitzgerald, who was perhaps a relative of her father. Their residence seems to have been at No. 14 Downing's Lane Kenmare.

After both her parents died during the Famine she was admitted into one of the workhouses in Kenmare and then selected to emigrate to Australia under the Earl Grey Scheme.

The girls were sent to Cork on the 27 October 1849 under the supervision of the schoolmaster. £30 was supplied for their journey, maintenance in Cork and passage to Plymouth. They were transported to Cork city by Jeremiah Lynch for two shillings and six pence each plus one shilling and six pence per box. He supplied four good horses and cars with tarpaulin and straw for the emigrants and one horse and car with tarpaulin for the boxes.

Mary Ann left from Penrose Quay, Cork and travelled to Plymouth where she boarded the *John Knox* and then sailed via the Cape of Good Hope, arriving in Sydney on 29 April 1850. She was aged eighteen [arrival record says 17] and an orphan and 'bodily health, strength and probable usefulness to the colony – GOOD. No complaints requiring treatment on the ship'.

There was an attempt to 'educate' the girls on board and schoolmaster J.J. Jones was employed to teach the girls to read and write, but he seems to have encountered a lot of opposition especially from the 'Cashel and Cork girls who refused to attend their studies on deck'.

Mary Ann was initially housed in Hyde Park Barracks, the Immigration Depot for single females. She found a placement with the well-to-do family of Captain John Scarvell and his wife Sarah at Clare House, Windsor in the Hawkesbury Region of New South Wales. She was probably employed as a domestic servant. The uneducated Mary Ann seems to have had difficulty with her employers who applied during August 1850 to the Magistrates Court in Sydney to terminate her indentures. Mary Ann was then obliged to return to the Hyde Park Barracks.

The *Sydney Morning Herald* of 26 August 1850 reported the following:

Irish Orphan Girls – Mary Connor, a girl of apparently 17 to 18 years of age, appeared on the complaint of Mr Sydney Scavell, on behalf of his father and mother, Captain and Mrs Scavell, to answer the charge of neglect of work, laziness, and insolence. In answer to the charge, she made a long rambling statement, but as she spoke with her teeth closed, we could only catch a word here and there; indeed, their Worships, although she was purposely brought close to them, could scarcely understand a word she said. The Bench, however, listened with great patience, and having gathered something of alleged ill-usage, proposed putting her upon oath; but previous to doing so, Mr Fitzgerald (who had come into the Court a short time before, asked if she knew the nature of an oath? To which she replied in the negative. Did she know what an oath was? 'NO'. The Bench finding that 10s odd were due her for wages, suggested that Mr Scavell should contribute that sum towards her to the place from whence she came, at the same time telling the girl that they could not compel Mr Scavell to do so, but it was a mere suggestion. This was most cheerfully agreed to by Mr Scavell. The indentures were, of course, cancelled. Mr Fitzgerald remarked, that during his whole career in his capacity as a magistrate, he had never met with such a lamentable case. It was truly lamentable to see a girl arrived at her apparent age come before that Bench and not known the nature of an oath! The Bench hopes that where she was going to she might have her mind enlightened by proper instruction, and thereby render her more sensible of her duties, and more anxious to perform them, if she should get another situation. The girl came by the 'John Knox'.

The opinion of Professor Trevor McClaughlin, Macquarie University of New South Wales regarding the court appearance of Mary Connor brought by her employer Captain Scavell is as follows:

The newspaper account is most interesting and can be read in a variety of ways. It is a good example of an 'innocent abroad'. Remember where she came from, the time she came, probably only speaking English as a second language, and she comes face to face with the judicial and other trappings of the dominant culture and makes her own stand against them. She probably comes out of that newspaper account looking better than her supposed social betters. Why didn't the court listen to her claim of ill-usage – because she was innocent enough not to understand the significance of an 'oath' in court? A travesty.

By the time Mary Ann came to Sydney, the domestic servant market had to some degree been saturated with the female orphans. The practice of the authorities was to send those whose indentures were cancelled to somewhere other than Sydney. Soon after, on 2 September 1850, the steamer *Eagle* delivered 15 'Orphan Girls' to Brisbane – it is a good possibility that Mary Ann was one of these girls.

Twelve months later the marriage of 40 year old George Hough and 19 year old Mary Ann was celebrated on 19 October 1851, at Pugin's Chapel (St Stephens) Brisbane, by Robert Downing, the Roman Catholic priest for the parish of Brisbane and Ipswich in the county of Stanley, New South Wales (before separation). This priest was from Kenmare and his father, Simon Downing, was Mary's former landlord. George gives his address on 19 October 1851 as 'Kilcou [Kilcoy?], Brisbane River'. The marriage certificate shows Mary Ann, from Brisbane, was a Roman Catholic and was illiterate as she, along with the two witnesses, used an 'X' to sign the document. The witnesses were John Flynn of Brisbane and Margaret Sleet of Brisbane River. Mary was still unable to write when she registered Georges's death in 1884 – again she used her mark.

Brisbane in the 1850s, with a population of 8,375, had all the crude, robust vitality of a frontier town. Horsemen, bullock-drivers and pedestrians formed the only traffic in the rutted dusty roads that served as streets. Teamsters camped at Hunter's Forge, near the present centre of the city. Lean and bearded horsemen came in from distant stations, some with hair long and uncombed like kindred characters from the American West, wearing floppy hats plaited from cabbage-tree palm. They carried pistols in their holstered belts and shotguns in their saddle scabbards, for the roads were infested with marauding Aborigines and time – expired convicts turned bushrangers. A popular place for revellers was St Patrick's Tavern. At the Treasury Hotel soldiers of the 50th Regiment of Foot, known as 'The Dirty Half-Hundred', forgathered and often brawled with seaman, using their belt buckles as weapons. Aborigines were still dangerous in and around Brisbane in the 1850s. They were allowed in town during the daytime, but after sunset were forbidden to pass the 'boundary posts'.

George Hough was born in Chester, England, about 1810. He was convicted on 3 August 1839 at the Denbigh Assizes of horse stealing. He was 28 years old and single at the time and gave his trade as horse breaker. He was sentenced to ten years and transportation to the colonies, along with 310 other convicts (302 arrived alive) aboard the *Maitland*.

He received his Ticket of Leave No 44/2599 dated 11 October 1844, but was arrested again for stealing in 1849 and received a sentence of months in jail. 'A Ticket of Leave allowed a convict to work for his own benefit and acquire property on condition that he must reside in the prescribed area, attend a muster every few months and attend church weekly.'

George may have worked at Sir Evan McKenzie's Station, Kilcoy (his marriage certificate gives his residence as "Kilcou"). The McKenzies were assigned five convicts, two of whom were Irish. They were hired in Sydney. George was employed as a labourer and timber getter.

George and Mary Ann seem to have settled at Ipswich on the Brisbane River where George worked felling timber. They then moved to Leichhardt St in Brisbane. During this time George and Mary Ann had two daughters born: Ellen Elizabeth (9 August 1852) and Mary Ann (7 May 1854).

George was arrested again in 1855, for stealing two pairs of socks, two pairs of trousers and two pillowcases from a washing line behind the North Brisbane Hotel. His excuse was that 'he lapsed into a state of thoughtfulness while in a state of intoxication'. However, he was still sentenced to one month's hard labour in Boggo Road jail. In spite of this and a couple more lapses there are indications that he still had a good reputation.

George converted to Catholicism and was baptised at St Stephen's Cathedral on 24 May 1863. Teresa 'Tess' was born at Fortitude Valley in 1865. They were at Fortitude Valley when Queensland was granted separation in 1859.

The *Brisbane Courier* carried the following articles in reference to George:

Mr. A. Martin

... offered a number of properties by order of Building Society No. 2. Of twelve lots, nine wore sold as -follows : .. ; lot 8,at the risk of George Hough, subdivision 6 of eastern suburban allotment 31, containing 16 perches, with a 3-room house, for 25 pounds, to George Winstone.

Thursday: George Hough was apprehended in the street, by Constable Boc, having in his possession a quantity of wearing apparel, etc. which appears to have been stolen from the premises of Mr. Bond, of the North

Brisbane Hotel, who identified the property. The articles had been hanging out to dry. The prisoner was committed for trial yesterday. (Saturday 30 December 1854)

George Hough was indicted for stealing some clothing, the property of Edward Bond, at Brisbane, on the 28th December, 1854. Guilty: one month's imprisonment. (Wednesday 13 June 1855)

£1 REWARD.
STRAYED from Fortitude Valley, on Wednesday, the 7th instant, a Dark Brown MARE, branded J1 near shoulder, on neck near side. GEORGE HOUGH, Fortitude Valley. (Thursday 14 February 1861)

The family were at Windmill Street, Fortitude Valley for the births of Katherine 1967 and Eliza Jane 1970. George is listed in 1868 as a carter in Windmill St. and in 1870 as a labourer. At one time he collected timber from Downfall Creek, Chermside. His two older daughters are said to have helped him in this occupation. William and Richard both became draymen like their father.

George died at home in Windmill Street on 26 June 1884 of Apoplexy at the age of 74 (his death certificate says 84 years). Mary Ann lived in the house at Windmill Street until her death from abdominal cancer on 19 November 1896. Her daughter Eliza Jane Smith, who lived next door in Windmill Street nursed her while she was ill, and registered the death.

IN THE SUPREME COURT OF QUEENSLAND

Mr. Justice Real.
In the WILL of MARY HOUGH, late of Fortitude Valley, Brisbane, In the Colony of Queensland, Widow, Deceased. Notice is hereby given that the ACCOUNT of ELIZA JANE SMITH, the Executrix In the above named estate, from the Thirteenth day of January, 1897, to the Twenty-seventh day of February, 1897, has This Day been filed in my Office, duly verified by the said Eliza Jane Smith. All parties claiming to be interested in the said estate are at liberty to inspect the said Account at my Office, in the Supreme Court-house, Brisbane, on or before WEDNESDAY, the

Seventh day of April next, and If they think fit to object thereto. Notice is also given that, whether any objection is taken to the said Account or not, I shall after the aforesaid day, proceed to examine and inquire into the said Account. Notice is further given that any person who may desire to object to the said Account, or any item or items therein, or the allowance to (the Executrix of a commission thereon, must before that day file in my Office a Memorandum to that effect.

Dated this Third day of March, A.D. 1897.

(L.S.) W. A. DOUGLAS,

Deputy Registrar.

Information about Mary Ann's life in Sydney was supplied by Dorothy Chambers in her family history, *The Hough & O'Connor Australian Family* (2001).

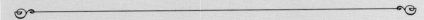

AN OPPORTUNITY
OR A TRAGEDY?

W HEN ONE TAKES into account the distress, sadness and despair that prevailed in Kerry during the Famine years, the poverty, privation and misery of the majority of the population prior to it and the continuing penury and destitution in the aftermath, there is no doubt that the Earl Grey Scheme was an opportunity for most of the girls who were 'selected' in Dingle, Kenmare, Killarney and Listowel.

An 'opportunity' is defined as a 'favourable chance' and we would have to agree that not all of the girls were capable physically or mentally of taking this 'favourable chance' and turning it to their advantage. We have to admire the physical strength of those girls who followed their husbands to the goldfields, trekking through unmade roads and rivers, evading bushrangers and aborigines, later having large families and living to a ripe old age.

There is no doubt from the histories here of a number of the girls, written by their descendants, that they were a brave, resourceful, spirited and gutsy set of women. They took on lives that demanded courage, extreme hard work, resilience in the face of misfortune, and were 'tough' in the best sense of the word.

In their lives as pioneering wives and mothers in the interior of New South Wales, in the goldfields and in the newly explored and discovered territory of Queensland, they showed a capacity to resist defeat, a strength of mind and body to take on demanding and dangerous challenges. While I have no evidence that any of the Kerry girls (with the exception of Margaret Raymond) suffered any mental traumas, we know that girls from other workhouses ended their lives in psychiatric institutions in Australia.

The tragedy or sadness and grief that must have been part of their experience would have sprung from the dislocation to such a different way of life. The Kerry girls, in the main, came to Australia from rural areas or the miserable dirty and overcrowded lanes of the towns. When 'volunteering' to travel halfway across the world, they had no idea of the way of life that was awaiting them and the displacement from the only life experiences that they knew from home.

In Kerry, they lived in large extended families, close together. Their entire worlds were their own townlands and maybe a few surrounding – as far as they could walk to or, if they were lucky, be taken in a donkey cart. Strangers, with the exception of authority figures, hardly ever ventured into their local territory. Their knowledge or experience of crops were limited to hay, wheat, corn, barley, turnips and potatoes. They were familiar with the domestic animals of dogs and cats, farm animals of pigs and hens, perhaps cows and sheep, and not much more. Their fires which were a constant feature of cottage life were sourced from local bogs. Rain and sunshine came in equal measures, the weather was never extreme. Floods and fires were almost non-existent.

While they lived a pauperised existence even before the Great Hunger, it was not all unhappiness and depression. A happy-go-lucky race, the long dark evening were spent sitting around the fire storytelling, fiddle and accordion playing, singing and dancing. Stories of the Fianna, the adventures of Diarmuid and Gráinne, tales of colossal hurling matches between the Fianna and the Tuatha de Dannan would have been passed on for generations from grandparents to children.

How did they cope with the loneliness of the bush, of the distances separating them not alone from their friends who had travelled with them, but the loss of connection with their extended kith and kin at home?

Irish families would have been deeply superstitious, they believed in the banshee and in fairies and all of the traditions and customs associated with keeping the fairies at bay. There wasn't a task in the house or at play that didn't bring a warning of what might happen if the fairies were crossed.

It was bad luck to put shoes on a table or chair, place a bed facing the door, bring hawthorn into the house, give a knife as a present, or wear green. And everyone knew that it would bring seven years' bad luck if they broke a mirror. The banshee and her wailing would definitely foretell a death and the belief was that it followed only some families. Who was there in Australia to listen to and sympathise with such beliefs?

The religious situation in Ireland, was one that could not be taken too earnestly at this time. Religious emancipation was granted in 1829 and it was from this time onwards that the Catholic Church grew its power. A lot of parishes did not have a church in the first quarter of the nineteenth century. Religion was generally passed on to the family by the mother or more so by the mother-in-law if she was also living in the home. Men did not overly concern themselves with the rituals. All would have observed the Friday abstinence and Lenten fasts, night prayers would have been said but attendance at Masses was not always possible.[1] It was difficult to travel to Mass in the churches that were scattered throughout the outlying areas. Large families meant that some of the family stayed at home from Mass to mind the younger ones.

The irony of the fear engendered in Australia that the Earl Grey girls would somehow set up a Papist state, now seems in hindsight a ridiculous supposition. In fact many of the girls married outside their faith within a very short time of arrival and they brought their children up as committed Christians in a number of different faiths.

On balance, we would have to say that the opportunity that these 117 girls were offered far outweighed the tragedy aspect.

We will leave the last word to the British Assistant Secretary to the Treasury, the infamous Charles Trevelyan, who stated in a letter in 1846:

> The judgment of God sent the calamity to teach the Irish a lesson, that calamity must not be too much mitigated ... the real evil with which we have to contend is not the physical evil of the Famine, but the moral evil of the selfish, perverse and turbulent character of the people.[2]

We know that these girls were neither 'selfish' nor 'perverse' but I like to think that they were 'turbulent' and remained so, in their new lives!

APPENDIX

ORPHAN DATABASE

SURNAME	CHRISTIAN	WRKHSE	AGE	NATIVE	SHIP	B CERT	PARENTS	FATHER	MOTHER	RELIGION	R/W ?
Barry	Mary	Dingle	16	C'Gregory	TA	Yes	Patrick/Ann	?	C'gregory	RC	Both
Brien	Mary	Dingle	16	Dingle	TA	?	James/Johanna	Dingle	?	RC	Read
Connor	Mary	Dingle	18	Dingle	TA	?	Thomas/Mary	Dingle	Dingle	RC	Neither
Dowd	Mary	Dingle	18	Dingle	TA	?	Michael/Johanna	?	Dingle	RC	Neither
Galvin	Ellen	Dingle	18	Dingle	TA	?	John/Mary	Dead	Dead	RC	Read
Griffin	Mary	Dingle	19	Ballyferriter	TA	Yes	John/Mary	?	Nr. Dingle	RC	Neither
Harrington	Julia	Dingle	16	C'gregory	TA	Yes	Patk/Margaret	Dead	Dead	RC	Neither
Kearney	Mary	Dingle	14	Blasket?	TA	?	James/Catherine	Dead	Dead	RC	Neither
Kennedy	Catherine	Dingle	19	Brandon Bay	TA	None	Patrick/Ellen	Dead	Dead	RC	Neither
Kennedy	Mary	Dingle	17	Dingle	TA	?	Daniel/Debby	Dingle	?	RC	Neither
Kenane	Eliza	Dingle	17	Dingle	TA	?	Michael/Bridget	Dead	Dead	RC	Both
McGillicuddy	Ellen	Dingle	16	Dingle	TA	?	John/Mary	?	Dingle	RC	Read
McMahon	Mary	Dingle	17	Kerry	TA	?	Robert/Margaret	Dead	Dead	RC	Neither
Moore	Bridget	Dingle	15	C'Gregory	TA	?	Thomas/Mary	Dead	Dead	RC	Neither
Moore	Johanna	Dingle	17	Dingle	TA	?	Lawrence/Mary	Dead	Dead	RC	Neither
Moriarty	Catherine	Dingle	17	Dingle	TA	Yes	Maurice/Margaret	Dead	Dead	RC	Neither
Moriarty	Mary	Dingle	16	Dingle	TA	Yes	Maurice/Margaret	Dead	Dead	RC	Read
Sheehy	Ellen	Dingle	16	Dingle	TA	?	John/Ellen	Dead	Dead	RC	Neither
Sullivan	Mary	Dingle	18	Dingle	TA	?	Cornelius/Ellen	Dead	Dead	RC	Neither
Connor	Mary	Kenmare	17	Kenmare E.	JK	None	Edward/Mary	Dead	Dead	RC	Neither

SURNAME	CHRISTIAN	WRKHSE	AGE	NATIVE	SHIP	B CERT	PARENTS	FATHER	MOTHER	RELIGION	R/W ?
Corkery	Mary	Kenmare	17	Kenmare E.	JK	Yes	Cornelius/Catherine	Dead	Dead	RC	Neither
Cronin	Margaret	Kenmare	16	Templenoe E	JK	Yes	Myles/Honora	Dead	Dead	RC	Neither
Dineen	Mary	Kenmare	18	Kenmare	JK	None	Denis/Julia	Dead	Dead	RC	Neither
Downing	Catherine	Kenmare	16	Ballybog E.	JK	Yes	Daniel/Catherine	Dead	Dead	RC	Neither
Foley	Jessie	Kenmare	17	Kenmare E.	JK	Yes	Patrick/MaryAnne	?	Kenmare	RC	Both
Foley	Margaret	Kenmare	14	Kilgarvan E.	JK	Yes	Timothy/Mary	Dead	Dead	RC	Neither
Husband	Ann	Kenmare	17	Templenoe E	JK	None	William/Jane	Dead	Dead	C of E	Neither
Lovett	Ellen	Kenmare	14	Kenmare E.	JK	?	John/Ellen	Dead	Dead	RC	Both
Manning	Catherine	Kenmare	18	Templenoe E	JK	?	John/Catherine	Dead	Ded	RC	Neither
McCarthy	Ellen	Kenmare	18	Ballybog E.	JK	?	John/Matty	Dead	Dead	RC	Neither
McCarthy	Mary	Kenmare	18	Kilgarvan E.	JK	?	James/Mary	Dead	Dead	RC	Neither
McCarthy	Mary	Kenmare	16	Kenmare	JK	?	Thomas/Judith	Dead	Dead	RC	Neither
Murphy	Margaret	Kenmare	17	Tuosist E.	JK	?	John/Mary	Dead	Kenmare	RC	Neither
Murphy	Mary	Kenmare	16	Kenmare E.	JK	?	Denis/Eliza	Dead	Dead	RC	Neither
Reardon	Frances	Kenmare	17	Kenmare	JK	?	James/Fanny	Dead	Dead	RC	Both
Regan	Mary	Kenmare	16	Tuosist E.	JK	?	John/Kate	Dead	Dead	RC	Neither
Shea	Mary	Kenmare	18	Kenmare E.	JK	?	John/Honora	Dead	Dead	RC	Neither
Shea	Julia	Kenmare	17	Bonane E.	JK	?	Denis/Mary	Dead	Dead	RC	Neither
Shea	Jane	Kenmare	19	Ballybog E.	JK	?	John/Margaret	Dead	Dead	RC	Neither
Shea	Mary	Kenmare	18	Tuosist E.	JK	?	Patrick/Margaret	Dead	Dead	RC	Neither

SURNAME	CHRISTIAN	WRKHSE	AGE	NATIVE	SHIP	B CERT	PARENTS	FATHER	MOTHER	RELIGION	R/W ?
Sullivan	Mary	Kenmare	17	Tuosist E.	JK	?	Sylvester/Mary	Dead	Dead	RC	Neither
Sullivan	Catherine	Kenmare	18	Kenmare E.	JK	?	Daniel/Ellen	Kenmare	Kenmare	RC	Neither
Sullivan	Honora	Kenmare	18	Tuosist E.	JK	?	Denis/Honora	Dead	Dead	RC	Neither
Sullivan	Margaret	Kenmare	20	Kilgarvan E.	JK	Yes	Connor/Mary	Dead	Dead	RC	Neither
Doherty	Honora	Killarney?	16	Killarney	EN	Yes	John/Johanna	?	?	RC	?
Donoghue	Johanna	Kilarney?	14	Killarney	EN	Yes	Thomas/Johanna	?	?	RC	?
Donovan	Ellen	Killarney?	19	Killarney	EN	Yes	Denis/Ellen	?	?	RC	?
Doody	Mary	Killarney?	18	Ballydribbeen	EN	Yes	William/Julia	?	?	RC	?
Foley	Bridget	Killarney?	15	Ballydrisheen	EN	Yes	Michael/Mary	?	?	RC	?
Healy	Mary	Killarney	14	Killarney	EN	Yes	Jeremiah/Ellen	?	?	RC	?
Hegarty	Catherine	Killarney?	17	Killarney	EN	Yes	Denis/Mary	?	?	RC	?
Leary	Ellen	Killarney	17	Islandmore	EN	Yes	Daniel/Julia	?	?	RC	?
McCarthy	Honora	Killarney?	19	Aghucureen	EN	Yes	Timothy/Bridget	?	?	RC	?
McCarthy	Catherine	Killarney?	14	Gortroe	EN	Yes	Timothy/Catherine		?	RC	?
McCarthy	Ellen	Killarney?	18	Allanes Glens	EN	Yes	Daniel/Ellen	?	?	RC	?
Mangan	Honora	Killarney?	15	Inchanagh	EN	Yes	Owen/Mary	?	?	RC	?
Moriarty	Johanna	Killarney?	16	Crohane	EN	Yes	Daniel/Mary	?	?	RC	?
Riordan	Ellen	Killarney	19	Killarney	EN	?	?	?	?	RC	?
Powell	Ellen	Killarney	19	Killarney	EN	Yes	John/Catherine	?	?	RC	?
Smyth	Johanna	Killarney?	19	Killarney	EN	Yes	James/Catherine	?	?	RC	?

SURNAME	CHRISTIAN	WRKHSE	AGE	NATIVE	SHIP	B CERT	PARENTS	FATHER	MOTHER	RELIGION	R/W ?
Brandon	Mary	Listowel	16	Newtownsandes	TA	None	Thomas/Mary Anne	Dead	Dead	RC	Both
Casey	Ellen	Listowel	17	Ratoo	TA	Yes	Patrick/Elizabeth	Dead	Dead	RC	Both
Casey	Mary	Listowel	16	Duagh	TA	Yes	Timothy/Ellen	?	Listowel	RC	Both
Connor	Margaret	Listowel	18	Listowel	TA	Yes	James/Anne	Dead	Dead	RC	Both
Conway	Mary	Listowel	17	Dromkeen E.D	TA	None	Robert/Mary	Dead	Dead	RC	Neither
Hayes	Johanna	Listowel	15	Lixnaw	TA	Yes	William/Mary	Dead	Listowel	RC	Neither
Jones	Hanna	Listowel	16	Listowel	TA	None	John/Ellen	Dead	Dead	RC	Both
Pierse	Winnie	Listowel	19	Ballyduff	TA	Yes	David/Ellen?	Dead	Dead	RC	Neither
Purcell	Mary	Listowel	18	Listowel	TA	Yes	James/Honora	Dead	Dead	RC	Both
Raymond	Margaret	Listowel	18	Listowel	TA	None	William/Honora	Dead	Dead	RC	Both
Ryan	Catherine	Listowel	19	Tarbert	TA	Yes	Michael/Margaret	Dead?	Dead	RC	Both
Ryan	Biddy	Listowel	16	Bruff, Co. Limk	TA	None	Anthony/Johanna	Sydney	?	RC	Both
Ryan	Mary	Listowel	17	Abbeydorney	TA	Yes	John/Catherine	Sydney	?	RC	Both
Scanlon	Margaret	Listowel	16	Listowel	TA	Yes	James/Honora	Dead	Dead	RC	Both
Wilson	Ellen	Listowel	19	Listowel	TA	None	Thomas/Hanora	Dead	Dead	C of E	Both
Wilson	Mary	Listowel	16	Listowel	TA	None	Thomas/Hanora	Dead	Dead	C of E	Both
Buckley	Nancy	Listowel	19	Listol (sic)	TS	None	John/Margaret	Dead	Dead	RC	Neither
Burrian	Margaret	Listowel	16	Listowl (sic)	TS	None	Patrick/Mary	?	Listowel	RC	Both
Connor	Kate	Listowel	18	Rathguire?	TS	None	Edward/Julia	Dead	Dead	RC	Neither
Connor	Margaret	Listowel	17	Ballylongford	TS	None	Thomas/Catherine	Dead	Dead	RC	Read

SURNAME	CHRISTIAN	WRKHSE	AGE	NATIVE	SHIP	B CERT	PARENTS	FATHER	MOTHER	RELIGION	R/W ?
Courtney	Mary	Listowel	19	Rattoo	TS	?	Denis/Honora	Dead	Ratoo	RC	Read
Creagh	Mary	Listowel	18	Listowel	TS	Yes	Patrick/Ellen	Dead	Dead	RC	Read
Daly	Julia	Listowel	18	Tralee	TS	Yes	Henry/Elizabeth	Dead	Dead	C of E	Both
Daly	Mary	Listowel	17	Listowel	TS	?	John/Bridget	?	L. Union	RC	Neither
Griffin	Bridget	Listowel	19	Listowel	TS	?	John/Johanna	Dead	Dead	RC	Neither
Ginniew	Margaret	Listowel	18	Stow	TS	?	James/Mary	Dead	Dead	RC	Read
Kissane	Deborah	Listowel	18	Listowl (sic)	TS	?	John/Mary	Dead	Dead	RC	Both
Leary	Ellen	Listowel	16	Ardfert	TS	?	James/Hanora	Dead	Dead	RC	Neither
Mallowney	Catherine	Listowel	19	Millstreet	TS	Yes	William/Hanora	Kerry	Dead	RC	Read
O'Brien	Honora	Listowel	19	Listowel	TS	?	Patrick/Ellen	Dead	Dead	RC	Neither
Relihan	Ellen	Listowel	19	Listowel	TS	?	John/Mary	?	Listowel	RC	Neither
Scanlon	Johanna	Listowel	18	Listowel	TS	?	Michael/Mary	Dead	Dead	RC	Read
Stack	Mary	Listowel	18	Kilmore	TS	?	James/Margaret	Dead	Dead	RC	Read
Sullivan	Catherine	Listowel	19	Listowel	TS	?	Denis/Mary	Dead	Dead	RC	Neither
Sullivan	Johanna	Listowel	14	Dwyer	TS	?	Charles/Mary	Dead	Dead	RC	Both
Sullivan	Mary	Listowel	16	Beale	TS	?	John/Hanora	?	Listowel	RC	Neither

NOTES

Chapter 1

1. Jeremiah King, *County Kerry, Past and Present*, a handbook to the local and family history of the county, (Cork 1986), p. 111.
2. Kerry Census figures http://www.kerrycdb.ie/kerryanalysis/population.pdf accessed 10 December 2012.
3. Devon Commission Report, Part 11, p. 1,152.
4. Cormac Ó Gráda, *Ireland's Great Famine, An Overview* (University College Dublin, Centre for Economic Research, Working Paper Series, 2004).
5. Ibid.
6. Arthur Young, *A Tour in Ireland* (Dublin 1780), Vol. 2, p. 43.
7. John Pierse, *Teampall Bán* (Listowel 2013).
8. Joel Mokyr, *Why Ireland Starved* (London 1983), p. 87.
9. Ibid., p. 202.
10. Gaughan, J. Anthony, *Listowel and its Vicinity* (Leinster Leader Naas, 1974), p. 146.
11. William J. Smyth, *Atlas of the Great Irish Famine, Variations in Vulnerability* (Cork University Press 2012), p. 187.
12. Gustave de Beaumont, *Ireland: Social, Political, and Religious*, W.C. Taylor (ed.) (London: Richard Bentley, 1839), 2 vols, Vol. 1, p. 266.
13. Bertie O'Connor-Kerry, *Slieveadara School, 150 Years of Official Education* (Ballyduff Magazine 1994), p. 5.
14. Ibid.
15. De Moleyns to Relief Commission, 25 May 1846, as quoted Kieran Foley, 'The Famine in the Dingle Peninsula' in *Atlas of Great Irish Famine* (Cork 2012), p. 398.

16 De Moleyns to Relief Commission, 25 May 1846, as quoted Kieran Foley, 'The Famine in the Dingle Peninsula' in Atlas of Great Irish Famine (Cork 2012), p. 398.

17 *The Times*, 6 January 1849.

18 http://landedestates.nuigalway.ie/LandedEstates/jsp/estate-show.jsp?id=1859, accessed 25 February 2013.

19 Shane Lehane, 'Matthew Trant Moriarty and the Famine in Ventry', *The Famine in Kerry*, Michael Costello (ed.) (KAHS Tralee 1997), p. 59.

20 Ibid., p.61.

21 *Kerry Examiner*, 8 February 1847.

22 *Kerry Evening Post*, 30 January 1847; 'The Great Famine', cited in Shane Lehane MA Thesis, 2005.

23 Landed Estates Database, NUI Galway.

24 Gerard J. Lyne, *The Landsdowne Estate in Kerry under W.S. Trench 1849–1872* (Dublin 2001), p. 3.

25 Devon Comm.Ev., ii, p.143, q.2686 quoted in Lyne, *The Landsdowne Estate in Kerry under W.S. Trench 1849-1872* (Dublin 2001).

26 Famine Account as described on plaque in Old Kenmare Cemetery.

27 W.S. Trench, *Realities of Irish Life* (London 1869), p. 113.

28 Landed Estates Database, NUI Galway (Estate Browne Kenmare).

29 Rental of Earl of Kenmare Estate, 1830–1850 (PRONI accessed 21 June 2013).

30 Ibid.

31 *Tralee Chronicle*, July 1848.

32 *Slaters Commercial Directory*, 1846.

33 *Limerick Chronicle*, Wednesday 12 July 1837 (Vol. 71).

34 Kieran O'Shea, *The Diocese of Kerry*, Formerly Ardfert (Strasbourg 2005), p. 97.

35 http://www.slsa.sa.gov.au/fh/passengerlists/1849elgin.htm.

36 Death certificate in 1902 states '3 years in SA and 47 years in Vic'.

37 John Pierse, *Teampall Bán* (Listowel 2013).

38 Tim P. O'Neill, *Famine, Land and Culture in Ireland*, Carla King (ed.) (UCD Press Dublin, 2000).

39 *The Journals of Sir John Benn Walsh*, James S. Donnelly Jnr (ed.); *Journal of the Cork Historical and Archaeological Society*, Jul–Dec 1974, Jan–Jun 1975.

40 Fr Matthias McMahon letter to *The Nation*, 28 April 1850.

41 Ibid.

42 M.G. Moyle and de Brún, P., 'Charles O'Brien's Agriculture Survey of Kerry, 1800', *Journal of the Kerry Archaeological and Historical Society*, No. 1, pp. 73-100, No. 2, pp. 108–132, 1968–69.

43 Cecil Woodham-Smith, *The Great Hunger Ireland 1845–1849* (London 1991), p. 75.

Chapter 2

1 Peter Higginbotham, *The Workhouse in Ireland*, accessed 2 July 2013 http://www.workhouses.org.uk/Ireland/.

2 Ibid.

3 1 & 2 Vic. C.56 An Act for the more effectual relief of the Destitute Poor in Ireland *British Parliamentary Papers*.

4 Poor Law Commissioners, State of the Unions in Ireland, http://eppi.dippam.ac.uk/documents/12269/eppi_pages/296037 accessed February 2013.

5 Brid A. Liston, *Education in Listowel Workhouse 1845–1859*, Research Project, Education Department, Mary Immaculate College, Limerick, quoted in John Pearse, *Teampall Bán* (Listowel 2014).

6 Noel Kissane, *The Irish Famine, A Documentary History* (National Library of Ireland 1995), p. 101.

7 Fr Kieran O'Shea, 'In the Line of Duty', in *The Famine in Kerry*, Michael Costelloe (ed.) (KAHS Tralee 1997), pp. 28–30.

8 Ibid., pp. 56–57.

9 Ibid., p. 57.

10 Sr Philomena McCarthy, *Kenmare and its Storied Glen* (Killarney 1993), p. 66.

11 Diary of Fr John Sullivan, Kerry Diocesan Archives, Killarney.

12 Fr Kieran O'Shea, 'In the Line of Duty', in *The Famine in Kerry*, Michael Costelloe (ed.) (KAHS Tralee 1997), p. 30.

13 William J. Smyth, 'The Province of Munster and Great Famine' in *Atlas of Great Irish Famine* (Cork 2012), p. 369.

14 Ibid.

15 John Pierse, *Teampall Bán* (Listowel 2013).

16 Ibid.

17 Smith's *History of Kerry*, indicates that Lancelot Sandes was granted an estate in Kerry in 1667 under the Acts of Settlement. The estate of Charles L. Sandes was one of the principal lessors in the parish of Aghavallen, barony of Iraghticonnor, at the time of Griffith's Valuation. *The Ordnance Survey Name Book* noted in the 1830s that he held lands from the Trinity College estates. William Sandes held several townlands in the parishes of Kilnaughtin, Knockanure and Murher, in the same barony. In 1863, 1864 and 1865, over 2,000 acres of William Sandes estate was offered for sale in the Landed Estates Court.

Chapter 3

1 'Immigration', *Sydney Herald* (NSW: 1831–1842) 28 June 1838: 4. Web. 14 Aug 2013 http://nla.gov.au/nla.news-article12862413.

2 'The Colonist', *The Colonist* (Sydney, NSW: 1835–1840) 22 September 1840: 2. Web. 12 Aug 2013 http://nla.gov.au/nla.news-article31725656.

3   'The Colonist', *The Colonist* (Sydney, NSW: 1835–1840) 22 September 1840: 2. Web. 12 Aug 2013 http://nla.gov.au/nla.news-article31725656.

4   Ibid.

5   Judith Iltis, 'Chisholm, Caroline (1808–1877)', *Australian Dictionary of Biography*, National Centre of Biography, Australian National University, http://adb.anu.edu.au/biography/chisholm-caroline-1894/text2231, accessed 12 August 2013.

6   Joseph Robins, *The Lost Children: The Workhouse Child 1840–1860*, p. 199.

7   Judith Iltis, 'Chisholm, Caroline (1808–1877)', *Australian Dictionary of Biography*, National Centre of Biography, Australian National University, http://adb.anu.edu.au/biography/chisholm-caroline-1894/text2231, accessed 12 August 2013.

8   'Review', *Australasian Chronicle* (Sydney, NSW: 1839–1843) 6 September 1842: 2. Web. 12 August 2013 http://nla.gov.au/nla.news-article31737084.

9   D.W.A. Baker, 'Lang, John Dunmore (1799–1878)', *Australian Dictionary of Biography*, National Centre of Biography, Australian National University, http://adb.anu.edu.au/biography/lang-john-dunmore-2326/text2953, accessed 14 August 2013.

10 Mary Durack, *Kings in Grass Castles* (Australia 1997), p. 369.

11 Ibid., p. 369.

12 'The Darling Downs Early Pastoral Settlement', *Townsville Daily Bulletin* (Qld. : 1885 - 1954) 15 Aug 1952: 5. Web. 25 Oct 2013 http://nla.gov.au/nla.news-article63540602.

13 Thomas Spring-Rice, Monteagle – Papers [M976], 1833–1857 Library of New South Wales.

14 British Parliamentary Papers relative to Emigration to the Australian Colonies, (London 1848), p. 3.

15 Ibid., p. 14.

16 Edward Senior evidence to Select Committee on Poor Laws (Ireland), Third Report p.113.

17 Ibid., p. 113.

18 Edward Senior evidence to Select Committee on Poor Laws (Ireland), Third Report, pp.113–114.

19 British Parliamentary Paper, Papers Relative to Emigration, p. 83.

20 Ibid., p. 88.

21 Ibid., p. 88.

22 Robins, *The Lost Children*, pp. 176-270.

23 Ibid., p. 179.

24 Apendix to the First Annual Report, p. 96.

25 Ibid., p. 96.

26 Joseph Robins, *The Lost Children*, p. 201.

27 *Sydney Morning Herald* (NSW), 3 March, p. 5, viewed 25 November, 2013, http://nla.gov.au/nla.news-page1503148.

Chapter 4

1 *Tralee Chronicle*, 7 April 1849, quoted in Kieran Foley, 'Kerry During the Great Famine', Unpublished Phd Thesis, UCD 1997, p. 294.

2 Ibid.

3 *The Nation*, 26 February 1848, quoted in O'Farrell, *The Irish in Australia 1788 to the Present* (Cork University Press 1966), p. 74.

4 Ibid.

5 Third Report from Select Committee on Poor Laws, p. 157.

6 Letter from Poor Law Commission Office, Dublin sent to the Clerk of each Union entitled Emigration of Orphans from Workhouses in Ireland, 7 March 1848 Appendix (ii).

7 Letter from W. Stanley, Secretary to Poor Law Commissioners, 7 March 1848.

8 Minutes of Board of Guardians Killarney Workhouse Union, 29 April 1848 (held in Kerry Local History Library, Tralee).

9 Ibid., 29 January 1849.

10 Ibid., 13 February 1849.

11 Ibid., 2 May 1849.

12 1849 'Shipping Intelligence', *South Australian Register* (Adelaide, SA: 1839–1900), 12 September, p. 3, viewed 15 October, 2013, http://nla.gov.au/nla. news-article50247741.

13 Ibid., 28 March 1849.

14 Ibid., 19 October 1849.

15 'The method of selection adopted by him was a simple one. As the girls sat in the workhouse refectory he walked amongst them making his choice.' 'Irish Orphan Emigration to Australia 1848-1850' by Joseph A. Robins in *Studies: An Irish Quarterly Review*, Vol. 57, No. 228 (Winter 1968).

16 Minutes of Listowel Board of Guardians, 12 September 1849 (held in Kerry Local History Library, Tralee).

17 Minutes of Board of Guardians Listowel Union Workhouse, 12 September 1849 (held in Local History Section Tralee Library).

18 Ibid., 11 October 1849.

19 *Kerry Examiner*, 8 February 1847.

20 Captain Hotham to the Commissioners, 4 January 1848, Poor Law Commissioners, *Papers relating to the relief of distress*, p. 300.

21 Minutes of Board of Guardians Dingle Workhouse 17 March 1849 (held in Kerry Local History Library, Tralee).

22 Ibid., 22 September 1849.

23 Ibid., 15 September 1849.

24 Ibid., 5 October 1849.

25 Ibid., 10 October 1849.

26 *London Illustrated News*, October 1849.

27 Minutes of Board of Guardians Eingle Union Workhouse, 6 November 1849 (held in Local History Section, Tralee Library), 70/353.

28 Gray, *Famine Land & Politics*, p. 62-5, quoted in Gerard J. Lyne, *The Landsdowne Estate in Kerry under the agency of William Steuart Trench 1849–72* (Dublin 2001), p. xxxii.

29 Ibid., p. xxxv.

30 Ibid., p. xxxv.

31 Gerard J. Lyne, *Taylors of Dunkerron*, in Journal of KAHS No. 17, 1984, p. 72.

32 Minutes Kenmare Board of Guardians, Wednesday 29 August 1849, p. 82 (held in Kerry Local History Library, Tralee).

33 Ibid., 22 September 1849.

34 Minutes Kenmare Board of Guardians, Wednesday 31 October 1849, p. 186 (held in Kerry Local History Library, Tralee).

35 Ibid., 12 November 1849.

36 Ibid., 17 November 1849.

37 William Steuart Trench, *Realities of Life* (Longmans, London 1869), p. 116.

38 Ibid.

39 Minutes Kenmare Board of Guardians, 29 November 1849.

40 Ibid.

41 Trevor McClaughlin, History Ireland, Accessed online http://www.historyireland.com/volumes/volume8/issue4/features/?id=245, 3 January 2013.

42 Christine Kinealy, *This Great Calamity, The Irish Famine 1845–52* (Dublin 1994, 2006), p. 324.

43 Joseph Robins, *The Lost Children: A Study of Charity Children in Ireland 1700–1900* (Dublin: Institute of Public Administration 1980), p. 208.

44 The Tithe Applotment Books are a vital source for genealogical research for the pre-Famine period/ They were compiled between 1823 and 1837 in order to determine the amount, which occupiers of agricultural holdings over one acre should pay in tithes to the Church of Ireland (the main Protestant church and the church established by the State until its dis-establishment in 1871). There is a manuscript book for almost every civil (Church of Ireland) parish in the country giving the names of occupiers of each townland, the amount of land held and the sums to be paid in tithes.

45 Minutes of Listowel Board of Guardians, 7 March 1850 (Kerry County Library, Tralee).

46 http://www.thenoones.id.au/08_CATH_SHIP/cath_ship.html.

Chapter 5

1 Minutes of Listowel Board of Guardians, 22 March 1851 – reproduced from John Pierse, *Teampall Bán* (Listowel 2013).

2 Killarney Board of Guardian Minutes, 10 June 1848 (Kerry Local History Section Tralee Library).

3   John Grenham, *Tracing Your Irish Ancestors* (Dublin 2012), p. 7.

4   The Killarney girls have not been included so far (January 2013).

5   http://www.scoilnet.ie/womeninhistory/content/unit3/WomenInWorkhouses. html.

6   Joseph Robins, *The Lost Children*, p. 274.

7   Dympna McLoughlin, 'The Impact of the Great Famine on subsistent Women' in *Atlas of the Great Irish Famine*, p. 261.

8   Emigration Commissioners to Colonial Department, 17 February 1848, *First Annual Report 1848*, pp.151–152.

9   *Australian Dictionary of Biography*.

10 Reg. 2 No. 296, 2 March 1850.

11 *Limerick Chronicle*, 12 July 1837, p. 2.

12 https://sites.google.com/a/aotea.org/don-armitage/Home/great-barrier-island-history/captjeremiah-w-nagle-1802-1882/convicts-on-the-neptune-1837-8-commanded-by-nagle.

13 *Sydney Morning Herald* (NSW: 1842–1954), Thursday 19 September 1850, p. 3.

14 Goodbody, Rob, *Limerick Quakers & Famine Relief, Old Limerick Journal* No. 25.

15 S.M. Ingram, *Enterprising Migrants*, An Irish Family in Australia, (Melbourne 1975), p. 148.

16 Trevor McClaughlin, *Barefoot & Pregnant?*, Vol. 2 (Melbourne), p. 123.

17 Ibid., p. 123.

18 *Freemans Journal*, Dublin, 16 July 1839, p. 4.

Chapter 6

1   Tenth General Report of the Colonial Land and Emigration Commissioners, Appendix No. 7, p. 42.

2   *Ibid.*

3   Colonial Land and Emigration Commissioners Tenth Report, Appendix 1, p. 43.

4   Letter from W. Stanley, Secretary PLC to T.N. Reddington, Dublin Castle, quoted in Trevor McClaughlin, *Barefoot & Pregnant?* (Melbourne, 2001), p. 9.

5   Ibid.

6   Thomas Keneally, *The Great Famine and Australia*, p. 553.

7   *South Australian Register* (Adelaide, SA 1839–1900), 12 September 1849, p. 2. Web. 28 August 2013. http://nla.gov.au/nla.news, p. 2.

8   Ibid.

9   Charles Edward Strutt, Journal, October 1849–May 1850 ..., State Library of Victoria, Manuscripts Collection, MS 8345. Strutt was on board the emigrant ships *St Vincent*, London to Sydney, and *Thomas Arbuthnot*, London to Sydney and return.

10 Strutt, Journal, p. 3.

11 Ibid., Tuesday 23 October 1849, p. 61.

12 Ibid., Saturday 27 October 1849, p. 61.

13 D.B. Waterson, 'Hodgson, Sir Arthur (1818–1902), *Australian Dictionary of Biography*, Australian National University, http://adb.anu.edu.au/biography/hodgson-sir-arthur-1155/text5963, accessed 15 July 2013.

14 Ibid., Thursday 1 November 1849.

15 Hodgson, 4 November 1849.

16 Ibid.

17 Strutt, Journal, 11 November 1849, p. 63.

18 *Charleville Times*, Brisbane, 24 October 1947, p.18.

19 'Passing of a Pioneer', *Brisbane Courier* (Qld 1864–1933), 1 April 1916, p. 12, viewed 19 November, 2013, http://nla.gov.au/nla.news-article20100448

20 Hodgson, 4 December 1849.

21 Ibid., 17 December 1849, p. 63.

22 Ibid., 25 December 1849, p. 66.

23 Strutt, Journal, Tuesday 25 December 1849, p. 67.

24 Hodgson, Saturday 12 January 1849.

25 Strutt, Journal, Monday 4 February 1850, p. 70.

26 Strutt, Journal, Friday 8 February 1850, p. 71.

27 *Sydney Morning Herald* (NSW: 1842–1954), 27 July 1850, p. 3, viewed 19 September 2013, http://nla.gov.au/nla.news-article12919795.

28 *Sydney Morning Herald* (NSW: 1842–1954), 30 April 1850, p. 2, viewed 18 September 2013, http://nla.gov.au/nla.news-page1511705.

29 *Sydney Morning Herald*, 30 April 1850, p. 2.

30 Research by Peter Noone, descendant of Catherine Noone's brother, Martin Noon. November 2012. http://www.irishfaminememorial.org/media/Noone_Catherine.pdf.

31 'Shipping Intelligence,' *Freeman's Journal* (Sydney, NSW: 1850–1932), 1 August 1850, p. 6, viewed 19 September, 2013, http://nla.gov.au/nla.news-article115767258.

Chapter 7

1 *Sydney Morning Herald* (NSW 1842–1954), 3 July 1850, p. 1, viewed 8 November, 2013, http://nla.gov.au/nla.news-page1511976.

2 Ibid.

3 *South Australian Register*, 23 October 1848, p. 2.

4 Ibid.

5 Ibid.

6 http://ehlt.flinders.edu.au/archaeology/department/publications/staniforth/2002e.pdf.

7 *Moreton Bay Courier* (Brisbane, Qld. : 1846 - 1861), 4 August 1849, p. 2, viewed 26 September, 2013, http://nla.gov.au/nla.news-page 2.

8   Christopher O'Mahony, *Poverty to Promise*, (Darlinghurst NSW 2010), p. 147.

9   National Archives of Ireland, http://www.nationalarchives.ie/wp-content/
    uploads/2012/03/Ireland-Australia-transportation.pdf., accessed 24 October 2013.

10 *South Australian Register* (Adelaide, SA: 1839–1900), 12 September 1849, p. 2,
    viewed 15 November, 2013, http://nla.gov.au/nla.news-page4148214.

11 http://landedestates.nuigalway.ie/LandedEstates/jsp/estate-show.jsp?id=1823
    accessed 20 September 2013.

12 '[No heading]', *South Australian Register* (Adelaide, SA: 1839–1900), 15
    September 1849, p. 4, viewed 21 September 2013, http://nla.gov.au/nla.news-
    page4148157.

13 1849 Elgin, Diane Cummings, http://www.slsa.sa.gov.au/fh/
    passengerlists/1849elgin.htm, accessed 20 September 2013.

14 'Criminal Jurisdiction', *South Australian Register* (Adelaide, SA 1839–1900), 20
    October 1849, p. 3, viewed 21 September, 2013, http://nla.gov.au/nla.news-
    article50247064.

15 Ibid.

16 'Police Court', *South Australian* (Adelaide, SA 1844–1851), 26 August 1850, p. 3,
    viewed 21 September 2013.

17 Ibid.

18 Strutt, Journal, p. 76.

19 Ibid., p. 73.

20 Ibid., p. 74.

21 Ibid., p. 74.

22 Ibid., p. 74.

23 Ibid., p. 75.

24 Ibid., p. 75.

25 Ibid., p. 75.

26 Ibid., p. 78.

27 Ibid., p. 78.

28 Ibid., p. 78.

29 Ibid., p. 80.

30 Ibid., p. 80.

31 Ibid., p. 90.

32 Ibid., p. 90.

33 *Sydney Morning Herald* (NSW 1842–1954), Thursday 19 September 1850, p. 3.

34 Dr Allen interviewed in his 93rd year in *Peeps into the Past, Pioneering Days on the
    Manning.*

35 http://www.australianhistory.org/goldfield-life, accessed 9 November 2013.

36 Christopher O'Mahony, Valerie Thompson, *Poverty to Promise* (Darlinghurst NSW
    2010), p. 22.

37 S.M. Ingram, *Enterprising Migrants – An Irish Family in Australia* (Melbourne
    1975), p. 148.

38 TrevorMcClaughlin,www.historyireland.com/volumes/volume8/issue4/
    features/?id=245 accessed 18 March 2013.
39 Bruce Mitchell, *The Australian Story & Its Background*, (Melbourne 1967), p. 89.
40 Ibid., p. 91.

Chapter 8

1   http://www.victorianweb.org/history/pms/dizzy.html, accessed 13 March 2012.
2   C. Woodham-Smith., *The Great Hunger: Ireland 1845–1849* (London 1962), p.
    36.
3   *South Australian Register* (Adelaide, SA 1839–1900), 13 March, p. 4, viewed 12
    November 2013, http://nla.gov.au/nla.news-page3932148.
4   *The Argus* (Melbourne, Vic.), Friday 15 March 1850, p. 2.
5   *South Australian Register* (Adelaide, SA 1839–1900), 13 March 1850, p. 4,
    accessed 26 September 2013, http://nla.gov.au/nla.news-page3932148.
6   Ibid.
7   Patrick O'Farrell, *The Irish in Australia, 1788 to the Present* (Cork University Press
    1966), p. 74.
8   Trevelyan to Clarendon, PROL T.64.367.C/I, 29 January 1848 quoted in Kinealy,
    This Great Calamity (Dublin 2006), p.317.
9   *South Australian Register* article (Adelaide, SA 1839–1900), Friday 6 January
    1854, p. 3.
10 Trevor McClaughlin, *Barefoot & Pregnant?*, Vol. 2, p. 119.
11 http://www.historyireland.com/20th-century-contemporary-history/lost-
    children, accessed 12 November 2013
12 http://en.wikipedia.org/wiki/Economic_history_of_Australia, accessed
    12 November 2013.

Conclusion

1   Erin I. Bishop, *The Work of Mary O'Connell 1778–1836* (Dublin 1999), p. 153.
2   Trevelyan, private letter to Col. Jones, 2 December 1846.

BIBLIOGRAPHY

Books

Beaumont, Gustave de (1839): *Ireland: Social, Political, and Religious*, ed. W. C. Taylor, London: Richard Bentley.

Butler, David J. (2006): *South Tipperary, 1570–1841. Religion, Land and Rivalry*. Dublin [u.a.]: Four Courts Press.

Coogan, Tim Pat (2012): *The Famine Plot, England's Role in Ireland's Greatest Tragedy*, N.Y.: Palgrave Macmillan.

Costello, Michael ed. (1997): *The Famine in Kerry*, Tralee Kerry Archaeological & Historical Society.

Crowley, John; Smyth, William J.; Murphy, Michael (2012): *Atlas of the Great Irish famine, 1845–52*. Cork, Ireland: Cork University Press.

Cusack, Mary Francis (1872?): *The Liberator, his life and times, political, social, and religious*. With an essay on the future of Ireland. London: John G. Murdoch.

Durack, Mary (1985): *Kings in Grass Castles*. Condell Park, AUS: Corgi.

Foley, Kieran (1997): *Kerry During the Great Famine, 1845–52*. Dublin: University College Dublin.

Gaughan, J. Anthony (1973): *Listowel and its Vicinity*. Cork: Mercier Press.

Gray, Peter (1999): *Famine, Land, and Politics. British Government and Irish Society, 1843–1850*. Dublin: Irish Academic Press.

Guerin, Michael (1996): *Listowel Workhouse Union*. Listowel, County Kerry, Ireland.

Hatton, Helen (1993): *The Largest Amount of Good, Quaker Relief in Ireland 1654–1921*, Quebec: McGill QUP.

Hughes, Robert (1987): *The Fatal Shore*, London: Pan Books.

Hurst, Michael (2002): *Political and Cultural Analysis of Ireland*. Bristol: Thoemmes.

Ingram, S.M. (1975): *Enterprising Migrants – An Irish Family in Australia*, Melbourne

Keneally, Thos. (1999): *The Great Shame*, London: Books.

Kinealy, Christine (1994): *This Great Calamity. The Irish famine 1845–1852*. Dublin: Gill & Macmillan.

Kinealy, Christine (1997): *A Death-Dealing Famine. The Great Hunger in Ireland*. Chicago, Ill: Pluto Press.

King, Carla (2000): *Famine, Land and Culture in Ireland*. Dublin: University College Dublin Press.

King, Jeremiah (1986): *County Kerry, Past and Present. A handbook to the local and family history of the county*. Cork: Mercier Press.

Kissane, Noel (1995): *The Irish famine. A Documentary History*. Dublin: National Library of Ireland.

Lyne, Gerard J. (2001), *The Landsdowne Estate in Kerry under W.S. Trench 1849–72*, Dublin, Geography Publications.

McClaughlin, Trevor (1991–2001): *Barefoot & Pregnant? Irish Famine Orphans in Australia*: documents and register. Melbourne: The Genealogical Society of Victoria (1,2).

McClaughlin, Trevor (1998): *Irish Women in Colonial Australia*. St Leonards, N.S.W: Allen & Unwin.

Mokyr, Joel (1983): *Why Ireland Starved. A quantitative and analytical history of the Irish economy, 1800-1850*. London, Boston: Allen & Unwin.

Moody & Martin (1994): *The Course of Irish History*. Cork: Mercier Press.

Morash, Christopher; Hayes, Richard (1996): 'Fearful Realities' in *New Perspectives on the Famine* edited by Chris Morash & Richard Hayes. Blackrock, County Dublin: Irish Academic Press.

McIntyre, Perry (2011): *Free Passage, The Reunion of Irish Convicts & their Families in Australia 1788–1852*. Dublin: IAP.

O'Brien, John B.; Travers, Pauric (1991): *The Irish Emigrant Experience in Australia*. Swords, County Dublin, Ireland: Poolbeg.

O'Connor, Joseph (1983): *Hostage to Fortune*. Tralee, County Kerry.: The Kerryman Ltd.

O'Farrell, Patrick (1966); *The Irish In Australia, 1788 To the Present*. Cork University Press.

O'Mahony, Christopher; Thompson, Valerie (1994): *Poverty to Promise. The Monteagle Emigrants, 1838-58*. Darlinghurst, NSW: Crossing Press.

O'Neill, P. (2000) Ed by Carla King, *Famine, Land and Culture in Ireland*, Dublin: UCD Press.

Phelan Rebecca; O'Brien, John B.; Travers, Pauric (1994/1991): *Irish Australian Studies*: Papers delivered at the seventh Irish-Australian Conference/The Irish emigrant experience in Australia. Sydney: Poolbeg.

Pierse, John, (2014): *Teampall Bán*, Listowel (as yet unpublished).

Reid Richard; Reid, Richard; Mongan, Cheryl (1996): *A Decent Set of Girls, The Irish Famine Orphans of the Thomas Arbuthnot, 1849–1850.* With assistance of Cheryl Mongan. Yass, New South Wales, Australia: Yass Heritage Project.

Robins Dr J.A. (1980): *The Lost Children: A Study of Charity Children in Ireland 1700 –1900.* Dublin: Institute of Public Administration.

Trench, W. Steuart (1966): *Realities of Irish Life.* With a preface by Patrick Kavanagh, etc. London (Fitzroy edition).

Woodham-Smith, C. (1991): *The Great Hunger: Ireland 1845–1849,* London: Penguin Books.

Young, Arthur (1970): *A Tour in Ireland, 1776–1779;* edited by A.W. Hutton. Shannon: Irish University Press.

Newspapers

Australasian Chronicle
Freeman's Journal (Sydney)
Kerry Examiner
Kerry Evening Post
London Illustrated News
Limerick Chronicle
Moreton Bay Courier
The Argus (Melbourne)
The Colonist (Sydney)
The Nation (Ireland)
The Times (London)
Tralee Chronicle
South Australian Register
Slaters' Commercial Directory 1846
Sydney Morning Herald

Parliamentary Papers

Commission on Occupation of Land (Ireland) known as Devon Commission Report, British Parliamentary Papers relative to Emigration to the Australian Colonies.
Tenth General Report of the Colonial Land and Emigration Commissioners 1850.
Third Report from Select Committee on Poor Laws in Ireland.
An Act for the more effectual relief of the Destitute Poor in Ireland 1838.

Journals, Diaries, Unpublished Theses

'The Journals of Sir John Benn Walsh' ed. James S. Donnelly Jnr *Journal of Cork Historical & Archaeological Society*, July–December 1974, January–June 1975.

Moyle, M.G. de Brún, P. *Charles O' Brien's agriculture survey of Kerry, 1800.* Journal of the Kerry Archaeological and Historical Society, No. 1, pp. 73–100, No. 2, pp. 108–132, 1968–.

O'Connor, Bertie, (1994), *Slieveadara School, 150 Years of Official Education,* Ballyduff Magazine 1994.

Lehane, Shane G., (2005), *The Great Famine in the Poor Law Unions of Dingle & Killarney, Co. Kerry, 1845–1852.*

Allen, Dr, interviewed in his 93rd year in *Peeps into the Past, Pioneering Days on the Manning.*

Charles Edward Strutt, Journal, October 1849–May 1850 ... State Library of Victoria, Manuscripts Collection, MS 8345.

Sir Arthur Hodgson Diary, Arthur Hodgson – Papers [M675, M789-790], 1838–1889 England–Australia per *Thomas Arbuthnot* 1849–50, National Library of Australia.

INDEX